RICKY GERVAIS

RICKY GERVAIS

The Story So Far . . .

MICHAEL HEATLEY

MICHAEL O'MARA BOOKS LIMITED

First published in Great Britain in 2006 by
Michael O'Mara Books Limited
9 Lion Yard, Tremadoc Road
London SW4 7NQ

A CIP catalogue record for this book
is available from the British Library

Hardback edition
ISBN: (10-digit): 1-84317-219-4
ISBN: (13-digit): 978-1-84317-219-2

Paperback edition
ISBN: (10-digit): 1-84317-237-2
ISBN: (13-digit): 978-1-84317-237-6

1 3 5 7 9 10 8 6 4 2

www.mombooks.com

Designed and typeset by Martin Bristow

Printed and bound in Great Britain by Clays Ltd, St Ives plc

Disclaimer
This book is an unauthorized account of the life of Ricky Gervais.
It has not been endorsed by either Ricky Gervais or his management.

The author and publishers are grateful to John Murray (Publishers) Ltd
for permission to reprint lines from 'Slough' by John Betjeman,
© The Estate of John Betjeman, from *The Collected Poems of John Betjeman*
(Murray, 1958; expanded, 1962).

Contents

Author Acknowledgements

As with my previous efforts for Michael O'Mara Books, fulsome thanks to Helen Cumberbatch and Lindsay Davies for their level-headed guidance and much appreciated advice. An enormous vote of thanks also goes to Nigel Cross, whose assistance on the analysis of Ricky's TV work was a key component of those chapters – despite a recent arrival in the family!

Alan Clayson, like Ricky a famous resident of Reading (Google 'Clayson and the Argonauts' for proof), was a great help in pinning down Ricky's early life and times.

Most information sources have been credited within the text, and my thanks goes to them, but two in particular need further mention: Elliott Day's excellent *Office* website www.wernhamhogg.co.uk, founded in February 2002, is a labour of love and, should Ricky revive the 'brand', may yet live again. Ben Walters's book *The Office* (ISBN 1844570916) in the BFI's TV Classics series was the first publication to zero in on Ricky's work, and is well worth seeking out.

Finally, while assistance was received from many 'off the record' sources, those who can be named as helpers in a small or large way include: Suresh Tolat, Deborah Kermode, Nephele Headleand, Georgie, Drew and Joe Heatley (Gervais fans one and all) and Hugh Fielder.

MICHAEL HEATLEY
August 2006

Photograph Acknowledgements

PAGE 1: Capital Pictures;
PAGES 2–3: © Fin Costello/Redferns (*all*);
PAGE 4: © geogphotos/Alamy (*above*),
© Steve Jennings/Corbis (*below*);
PAGE 5: Julian Makey/Rex Features (*above*),
Ian West/PA/Empics (*below*);
PAGE 6: Getty Images (*above*),
© Michael Putland/RetnaUK (*below*);
PAGE 7: Capital Pictures (*above*),
© Stan Kujawa/Alamy (*below*);
PAGE 8: Walt Disney/The Kobal Collection (*above*),
Rouge Pictures/Everett/Rex Features (*below left*),
© Touchstone/Everett/Rex Features (*below right*);
PAGE 9: © Craig Barritt/Retna Ltd;
PAGE 10: William Conran/PA/Empics (*above*),
Getty Images (*below*);
PAGE 11: Scott Myers/Rex Features (*above*),
Getty Images (*below*);
PAGES 12–13: Capital Pictures (*all*);
PAGE 14: Rex Features (*above*), Getty Images (*below*);
PAGE 15: Matt Baron/BEI/Rex Features (*above*),
Adam Houghton/Capital Pictures (*below*);
PAGE 16: Graeme Robertson/eyevine (*above*),
© Colin Bell/Corbis Outline (*below*).

Introduction

WHEN presenter of Radio 4's *Today* programme John Humphrys first became aware of Ricky Gervais, he hadn't watched television for nearly five years. Consequently, this made him one of the few people in Britain who failed to identify, in his words, 'a slightly demented-looking character with a beard', whose image adorned the cover of the programme for a business awards ceremony he was due to present at a posh London hotel. Thus, when Humphrys innocently enquired of his host whether the man in the photograph was the evening's 'big winner', a bemused silence followed. 'No,' came the astonished rejoinder. 'That's Ricky Gervais, possibly the biggest name on TV these days.'

When the two finally became properly acquainted some while later, Ricky greeted the story with an underwhelming, 'Oh . . . right.' While some would have raised a sarcastic eyebrow or perhaps taken mock offence, he didn't seem at all surprised that someone would choose to give television a miss. 'Being recognized is the worst bit of the whole package,' he told Humphrys in a *Radio Times* interview. 'It's very, very strange that people can be happy just from the recognition. I'm sick of the sight of my face, so Christ knows what other people think of it.' But despite playing down his star status, it's clear that the face of Ricky Gervais is one that discerning viewers certainly haven't tired of seeing on screen, particularly when it features in the award-winning comedies with which his name is now synonymous.

A private person who chooses not to embrace the celebrity lifestyle enjoyed by his peers – 'I don't go to premieres of films I'm not in. I don't do panel shows. I don't open supermarkets or go to showbiz events' – he prefers instead to spend time at home with Jane, his partner of more than twenty years, in front of the TV, away from the media spotlight. Nor is he ever likely to be found frittering away his fortune in boutiques frequented by the rich and famous; indeed the giant plasma screen adorning an entire wall of his flat is considered a rare luxury for someone disinclined to make the most of his new-found wealth.

Yet despite the loss of privacy associated with such public success, the man who came to the attention of the nation in his late thirties would acknowledge that his current status as Britain's most happening comic actor and writer is infinitely preferable to life as an entertainments officer at the University of London Students' Union. His time there in the 1990s was, he's since joked, mostly spent waving pieces of paper around and using the photocopier, but it set him up with plenty of source material for *The Office*, the 'docu-soap' TV series he both co-wrote with Stephen Merchant and memorably starred in as manager David Brent.

INTRODUCTION

The show, the first comedy classic of the current millennium, is already being talked of in the same breath as *Fawlty Towers* as an all-time masterpiece of British television. The problem – as many commentators have noted – is that when you've hit the bullseye with more or less your first dart, it sets an impossibly high standard for subsequent projects to meet. However, success was once again achieved by follow-up comedy *Extras*, another collaboration with writing partner Merchant, and the demand for his services as writer and actor, let alone the public's appetite for interviews, soundbites and personal appearances, has continued to be immense.

Before *The Office*, there had been a few sighting shots at the start of his foray into television, including an eponymous Channel 4 chat show, which may have gone unnoticed by the majority of his current admirers. Further to this, he had enjoyed a brief and inglorious career as a pop star, modelled on his musical idol David Bowie, video clips of which – to his chagrin – would pop up on many a *Before They Were Famous* TV compilation. Cheekbones more prominent, stomach less so, he was every inch the New Romantic, record sales apart.

Since hitting the nation's funny bone with *The Office* in 2001, Ricky has made a success of every new project in which he has been involved. From radio presenting to writing children's stories, stand-up comedy shows to charity work, providing voices for animated TV shows and films, and creating podcasts in the brave new era of downloading, no venture has proved too big or too small for Britain's most versatile entertainer.

This is his story so far.

1

The Road from Reading

❝ Dad was a labourer. Mum was a housewife.
It was probably quite a typical working-class childhood.
I was like a kid on tartrazine until I was sixteen. ❞

R ICKY DENE GERVAIS was born on 25 June 1961 in
Reading's Battle Hospital. He was never a Richard,
and the Dene, rather than Dean, is also unusual.

His parents Lawrence (known as Jerry) and Eva had
married in August 1944, Jerry having come over to
Britain during the war as a private in the Canadian army.
Though living in Ontario, the son of a farmer, he was of
French-Canadian stock, and Ricky typically makes light of
his French-English lineage. 'Bad breath and crap in bed,'
he has joked, calling it, 'the best of both worlds.'

Eva, the daughter of a tinsmith, was born and bred in
Reading and, at the time of her marriage, made her
living working for a printer's where she operated a paper-
folding machine. She was nineteen, and Jerry was six

years her senior. They met, so the story goes, during an air-raid blackout. In a rare in-depth interview in *The Guardian*, Ricky imagined his mum 'must have thought [Jerry] was glamorous for not having been born next door. And having the uniform and everything. Nearly as good as being a GI . . .'

As Ricky has explained, his dad's role in the war effort was actually far from glamorous or dangerous, but nevertheless important. 'He was [in] transport . . . He used to take tanks from the depot to the place they were needed.' (Indeed, Jerry's profession on his marriage certificate is stated as truck driver.) The family home was near a roundabout on Northumberland Avenue in Whitley, about a mile and a half from the centre of Reading. The estate was made up of council houses and would, in the 1970s, be the setting for an early TV docu-soap series *The Family* – an irony not lost on the creator of *The Office*.

Three children were born to Jerry and Eva before Ricky – Lawrence (known as Larry, in 1944), Marsha (in 1947) and Robert (known as Bob, in 1950) – so Ricky's appearance, more than a decade after the last, was somewhat unexpected. Like so many 'late arrivals', though, he not only benefited from the benevolent attentions of his elder siblings – reading, writing and telling the time came quickly – but he also enjoyed the more or less undivided attention of his mother, whose role in the lives of the older children was now undeniably less essential.

Mum Eva was by now a full-time housewife, who affectionately teased Ricky about the belated nature of his birth. 'My mum told me, "You was an accident," and I went, "Cheers!" Ha ha! A lot of honesty in my family.' He's likened them to fictional TV family the Waltons in that 'you had to answer back'. Being the youngest of the brood certainly encouraged him to fight his corner and attract the attention of his elders.

He's described his upbringing as 'nice' and 'normal', with no life-shaping traumas to recount. 'We lived on an estate, but I didn't have a deprived childhood. I was never hungry, always had clothes, but usually from a [mail-order] catalogue.' There's little doubt that its very ordinariness has helped Ricky keep his feet on the ground in the face of the temptations that stardom brings. That, and the fact that fame came later in life than planned. 'Everything I wanted as a kid, by the time I could afford it, I was forty,' he told *Q* magazine. 'So, unless you're Tom Hanks in *Big* or Jonathan Ross, you grow out of those things before you get enough money.'

Life on the drab housing estate in a three-bedroom house, with church, school and doctor's surgery in a convenient arc outside the front door, was nowhere near the poverty line, but the memory of labourer Jerry, who 'got up every day at 5.30 a.m., made a pot of tea and got picked up by a bloke in a van', has encouraged Ricky to appreciate at all times that he earns his livelihood doing what he enjoys. As he told *The Observer*'s Tim Adams in 2005: 'Being out of my comfort zone annoys me a bit; you know, if I have to drive a long way or something. Then I go: "Gervais. Your dad used to hod-carry. F**king grow up." That always tends to work.'

Eva, a former school dinner lady, did all the cooking at home, so Ricky didn't need to fend for himself too much until he finally flew the nest at eighteen. He later reminisced to *The Daily Telegraph*: 'When it was hot, she'd say, "Let's make a salad." A salad, growing up in my house, was egg, grated cheese, some lettuce and beetroot (which you left) and a bag of crisps. There were always chips on the go. And the king of meals – and it's still the king of meals – was the roast dinner. You can't beat it.'

As well as being an accomplished cook, Eva was also a seasoned wit, and one of her favourite sayings – 'What are you doing up so early? Shit the bed, have you?' – later turned up as a line spoken by a cleaner in *The Office*. Another was: 'You're about as much use as a one-legged man in an arse-kicking contest.'

Having learned to answer his parents and older siblings back – and more often than not getting a laugh out of it – Ricky was on the way to providing entertainment to the wider world. Not that everyone always saw the funny side: 'Mum was great fun, in that worrying way, whereas Dad was more cynical.'

Brother Bob, who also has a dry sense of humour, recalled in the *Daily Mirror* that Ricky 'was always showing off to get my mother's attention, but she was having none of it'. A childhood memory the two brothers share is being caught by Eva when they were secretly listening to Derek and Clive – Dudley Moore and Peter Cook's legendary expletive-filled 1970s alter egos. 'She panicked,' Ricky admits, 'but I think she liked it really. I think she thought it was quite funny and naughty. But all she could say was, "What if the vicar came around?"'

The Gervais residence had a pond in the garden and Eva hated her animal-obsessed eight-year-old bringing every possible life form in from it. As Ricky explained in a 2002 *Mirror* interview: 'Mum would say anything to make you feel the best. I love animals and we had a pond with frogs, toads, everything. She'd always be trying to throw the tadpoles away. One day I found a hedgehog that had drowned. I was really upset, but Mum just said, "He was probably diving in for those tadpoles."

'I love that,' he added, smiling at the memory. 'He's leaning in, going "mmm", and his mates are saying, "Leave it, Reg. You're not really seaworthy."'

Similarly, Ricky was indulged when it came to announcing his ambitions. 'Which was lucky,' he told *The Guardian*, 'because most kids have someone telling them not to be silly. An old auntie or someone saying, "Astronaut? Don't be a bloody fool, you're going into the fish factory."' At five he wanted to be a scientist, at seven a vet, at ten a marine biologist . . . The list went on and on.

He was also, and still remains, fascinated by gadgets. But the self-confessed geek has been disappointed with twenty-first-century technology which 'just hasn't kept pace with my needs. Where's the Individual Jet Pack that allows you to just take off and land somewhere else? Where's the Thought Downloader? The Moving Pavement? The Complete Meal In A Pill? As a child, I was told such things were just a matter of time . . .'

Family life certainly brought its share of laughs, and, as the 'baby' of the household, he quickly learned to give as good as he got when it came to dishing out insults. 'The whole point of my family was taking the mickey out of the one sitting next to you,' he revealed to *The Sunday Times*. 'That seemed to be the Reading way. It was all a wind-up. Everything was fine as long as you never got the hump.'

Ricky, who would later tape Eva for his radio show on Xfm, valued his mother's great working-class sense of humour: '[She had] an opinion on everything, and didn't mind what she said – as long as it wasn't in front of the neighbours.'

As his father was a lapsed Catholic, Ricky was encouraged to go to Sunday school, which he duly did from the age of five to eight. 'I had gold stars and used to win *Daniel in the Lion's Den* books, and everything was great. And I loved Jesus, I thought he was brilliant. What a great man.'

Then one day, his nineteen-year-old brother Bob came home and took a somewhat critical interest in his little brother's religious homework. According to a *Sunday Times* article, he decided to ask Ricky *why* he believed in God: 'And my mum got nervous. My mum went, "*Bob*" [delivered in a warning voice], and I thought, something's up. Then he went, "Well, what proof is there?" My mum said, "Of course there's a God." He went, "No, I'm just asking." And I said something ludicrous: "They've found evidence, they've found his blood in a bottle." I was just guessing. And Bob laughed. I could tell just by looking that he was telling the truth and my mum was lying. I knew the truth in that instant. That's why I put such a value in body language.'

His controversial declaration of atheism, aged eight, has been something he has never renounced. Yet Christmas was a festival much looked forward to, and as the kid of the family he was royally indulged. 'It's the one time of the year when everyone's a little bit nicer to each other,' he would later ruminate. 'I was allowed to eat sweets from about ten in the morning and then I'd run around like a maniac on sugar overload until I fell exhausted in a heap and was scooped up and put to bed. That was only until the age of fourteen, though.'

Thirty years on, people logging on to the London *Evening Standard* website would vote Ricky 'the ideal Christmas dinner guest'. In a poll to find 'the celebrity you would most like to tuck into the turkey with on Christmas Day', he romped home with 23 per cent of the vote, beating northern comedian Peter Kay and presenting duo Ant and Dec into second and third place respectively.

Ricky's most fondly remembered present from childhood was a cassette player he was given when he was nine – which, he soon found, offered much scope for playing pranks. 'I recorded a message saying, "Let me out of here! I'm running out of air!", hid it in my five-year-old nephew's wardrobe and pressed play. You should have seen his face . . .'

His early television viewing centred on cartoons. The sophistication of *The Simpsons*, of course, was many years distant, but he became a fan of animation from an early age: 'When I was at school and we had to write a story, everyone would write a story about going out or what they did, and I would do an original episode of *Tom and Jerry.*'

From 1966 to 1972 he attended Whitley Park infant and junior schools, a short walk away from his home. A school friend, Ricky Bell, recalls Gervais as being the class swot rather than the joker. 'He was . . . very academic,' he says. 'He didn't make everyone laugh that much at school – that humour came out later.' Even brother Bob has revealed, 'He was a goody-goody.'

He thrived at school, where he had many friends and loved learning 'because I was good at it and people were proud of me'. When his father died in 2002, he found some of the old school reports that had been kept. He later revealed to the *Mirror*'s Ryan Parry that 'they all say "disruptive" or "very good, but stops others" or "very good, but mucks around too much". My comedy has always been about showing off, taking the mick, which is still what I now do whether I'm on the telly, in the pub, or at home.'

Bob later found his kid brother's school report from when he was eleven: 'It was absolutely spot on, it was exactly as he is now. It said he was good at writing, acting and singing. He used to do all the school plays – he was a good actor.'

Although Reading is linked to London by an express railway and the M4 motorway, Ricky explained to *The Scotsman* that he rarely visited the capital in his youth: 'Maybe to the zoo a couple of times. I always knew I'd get out of Reading. I don't know why I was so sure about that, but I was.'

Holidays were modest affairs, as Ricky later revealed when he chose to consign caravanning trips to television's *Room 101*. He recalled taking his hols in a two-berth in Bognor with his mum and grandmother, and delighted viewers by sharing this unforgettable memory from holidays past: 'You have not known pleasure until you wake up in the middle of the night to the sound of your nan peeing in a tin bucket.'

As he entered his mid teens, holidays took second place to a holiday job – but working in a table-leg factory at sixteen didn't prove a barrel of laughs, as he revealed to the *Daily Mirror*. 'I had to take metal chunks out of a vat of oil and grind down their edges on a machine.' It did, however, provide him with 'the best piece of career advice I've had. On my first day, this bloke said, "Who are you trying to impress, mate? Why are you working so fast?"' His work ethic since then has been, 'Do the bare minimum and then complain you are overworked.' Another temporary job between school and university, as a gardener, brought in the princely sum (in those days) of £56 a week.

Much of that money was undoubtedly spent on long-playing records, because music was hugely important to the young Ricky Gervais. Indeed, he remembers the very first time he entered a record shop on his own with a £5 note in his hand – his objective, to buy an album. 'I must have been around twelve,' he recollected in *Mojo* magazine, 'and I was allowed into town by myself. There was a little trendy record shop upstairs at the Butts Centre in Reading that I thought was the coolest thing in the world because it was dark.'

He was to leave this dimly-lit emporium shortly afterwards, clutching either *Stranded* by Roxy Music or *Teaser and the Firecat* by Cat Stevens. His memory has played tricks . . . but the Roxy album's release date in December 1973, two years after the folky *Firecat*, nails it.

Even so, he believes the Cat Stevens album has worn better than its glam-rock rival. 'I think it's brilliant – it's honest and simple and melodic – but it's possible I'm just wallowing in nostalgia,' he mused to *The Guardian*'s Will Hodgkinson. 'Cat is not cool and he hasn't been since 1967, and then there's the whole Muslim thing – I have the feeling that people never forgave him for that . . .' Stevens turned to Islam in 1977, adopting the name Yusuf Islam and ceasing musical activity, but this posed no problems for Ricky.

'Lots of people won't listen to things that fall out of their remit of cool, but these so-called cool cats should listen to Cat Stevens's "How Can I Tell You" and tell me it's not lovely.' Indeed, it's said that Gervais, who has played Stevens's music on his Xfm radio show, was keen to use one of his lesser-known tracks, 'Sitting', as the theme to *The Office*. The significant final line of that song is: 'Just keep on pushing hard boy, try as you may/You're going to wind up where you started from.' In the end, of course, Mike d'Abo's maudlin 'Handbags and Gladrags' would be the favoured tune.

A soft spot for singer-songwriting was all very well, but Ricky's major idol of his early teenage years – and a daring one at that given his blue-collar environment – was gender-bending David Bowie. The face-painted, henna-haired singer's 1973 offering, *Aladdin Sane*, was to remain Gervais's favourite record for some two decades until it was superseded in 1995 by Radiohead's *The Bends*.

In an interview with *Zoo* magazine, he prized *Aladdin Sane*'s aura of 'melancholy beauty mixed with hope': 'Some would say this is pretentious but it's not – Robbie Williams is pretentious when he thinks he's writing profound lyrics and in fact he's just trying to find words that rhyme. Bowie is a brilliant singer, songwriter, musician. He's got it all.'

Indeed, David Bowie has remained the musician Ricky always wished he could be, and has also been a continued source of inspiration to him: he would go on to model his New Romantic pop persona on Bowie in the early 1980s; in 1998 his first self-penned foray into the TV world, *Golden Years*, would be based around the pop star and named after one of his songs. And it would be a huge thrill when, in 2006, his hero would agree to star in the second series of *Extras*.

Music and humour clearly played a big part in Ricky's life during his formative years. In the bosom of his family, joking was a survival skill and sulking a sin. As he revealed in *The Observer*, there was no time for teenage depression. 'I would never say: "What is the point of life?" I know there is no point to life. The point to life is having a laugh, getting on with everyone. Full stop.'

Surprisingly, perhaps, given the proliferation of bullies who feature in his work, Gervais was never a victim himself at school: 'I didn't know any.' But going one step too far and provoking a reaction is something he has always enjoyed doing. When he was a child in Reading, other kids, amazed by his cheek, regularly used to ask him if he'd been beaten up recently. And even today, 'People still say, "Gervais, how many times have you been punched in the face?"'

Having been able to walk to Whitley Park Primary, he now faced a longer trek on foot or a bus ride to Ashmead Comprehensive (now Thamesbridge College), which he would attend from 1972 to 1979. With longer distances to contend with, sensible footwear was a must, but as revealed to the *Times Educational Supplement* (*TES*) Ricky initially preferred to opt for fashion over practicality: 'I wore platforms to school for a while before I finally realized: God, this is so *uncomfortable*.'

Ricky was one of those rare children who enjoyed his schooldays and has only fond memories of this time of his life. Even so, he admitted to the *TES* that he dreaded 'winter mornings, when sometimes there would be ice on the inside of my bedroom window. I mean, actual sub-zero temperatures in my bedroom. I'd lie there dreaming I'd already got up and dressed. Then I'd wake for real, gutted. This was before central heating had reached Reading.' (He has never been a 'morning person', and now regularly schedules his business meetings for 11 o'clock or later.)

It was at Ashmead where Ricky first cultivated a reputation for being funny: 'It was a rough school, and humour was one way around that.' He himself admitted in *The Sunday Times* to being 'very uncool' and never so much as stole a packet of sweets from Woolworths – let alone a car, as seems to have been the fashion. 'I went to an all-boys comprehensive where you got detention for manslaughter and you had to kill more than five people before you got expelled. But I don't think I ever got into trouble. God, I am boring, aren't I?'

When homework allowed, he grew up watching classic British television comedy like *Porridge* and *Steptoe and Son*. 'There has always been something great to watch,' he told Bruce Dessau during a British Film Institute interview. 'Go back to the 1970s, there was loads I loved: *Fawlty Towers, Rising Damp, Porridge* . . .' Yet it was *M*A*S*H*, the US TV series of the movie about Korean War medics, which left him with a motto to live by when he was fourteen or fifteen. 'Hawkeye was going, "Look, we can't change the world, but we can change our corner of it." And that's absolutely stayed with me. What's that quote? "Honour is a gift a man gives himself." I *love* that.'

An earlier small-screen import of a military bent from the USA that also found favour with Ricky was *Sgt Bilko*. The description of the titular character, played by dome-headed comedian Phil Silvers, seems somehow familiar. 'He's pathetic, except you like him because he's a loser. And he's no threat. He's a middle-aged man . . . surrounded by idiots – waifs and strays – and he's got to look after them . . . I know we're looking at an antique,' Ricky concluded to *Uncut* magazine's Paul Lester in 2004, 'but it hasn't dated at all.'

Porridge, the prison comedy written by Dick Clement and Ian La Frenais, which starred Ronnie Barker, was, according to Gervais, '*Bilko* all over again – he's surrounded by idiots, but he's got to save them. And he's got to come out looking good . . . There's compassion there, and laughter in the face of adversity.'

Another favourite was *The Fall and Rise of Reginald Perrin* starring Leonard Rossiter (in Gervais's view, the greatest British sitcom actor): 'There's one lovely scene where Reggie's about to have an affair with his secretary Joan [played by Sue Nicholls] – I just realized I stole a bit of this, it's a bit David Brent – where he leans up against the wall, and gets a whiff of underarm and comes back down with a new shirt on. Then he does it again . . . That stayed with me for twenty-five years!'

Fawlty Towers, which Ricky has compared to a White-hall farce, 'but the best one ever', has often been likened to *The Office*, since creators John Cleese and Connie Booth decided to end the popular Torquay-based comedy after just two series, leaving the country wanting more. In Ricky's view, after waiting in vain over several years for some new episodes of the comedy, he doubted whether 'sitting down for the third series would have been as exciting as watching episode one of the second series'. Ricky himself drew a comparison between the

1970s programme and his own show on the subject of race, and the respective attitudes of the two main characters: 'It [*Fawlty Towers*] had that scene where he's in hospital and he [Fawlty] jumps back when he sees the black doctor. We did that in *The Office*, where Brent couldn't act normally around the black guy. It's about exposing prejudice.'

Aside from out-and-out sitcoms, Ricky was also tickled by the entertainment provided by the nation's favourites Morecambe and Wise, especially their running gags with classical pianist and conductor André 'Preview' Previn: 'Relationships are really important to me. I've always felt that comedy's contextual and that you've got to connect on an emotional level.' But when asked years later by a Scottish newspaper to populate an imaginary dinner party, Ricky's first choices remained his first- and best-loved comedy duo, Laurel and Hardy. Perhaps more surprisingly, he also cited 'my first hero, Muhammad Ali. There's no one like him.' Boxing would, startlingly, reclaim him as a participant rather later in life.

Back at Ashmead Comprehensive, the teacher who had the greatest influence on the young Gervais was English master Mr Taylor. 'He was cool, and that meant a moustache and a suit and tie,' he revealed in the *TES*. 'You never heard him coming because he wore Hush Puppies. This was the mid 1970s, remember.'

At that time English took very much second place to science in Ricky's list of priorities. But a maxim that the teacher tried hard to drum into the teenager – 'Write what you know' – would prove invaluable. Just as with the early *Tom and Jerry* episodes, whenever Ricky was asked to produce a story, he'd write 'as if for bad American television. At thirteen I did this story about a New York cop who shoots first and asks questions later. Mr Taylor gave it back: "B, too melodramatic." That's what he always said. My next story was about a kid in the Wild West who investigates a murder. He kneels on his friend's grave and shouts: "I will avenge thee!" Mr Taylor's mark: "B, too melodramatic. You've never been to the Wild West, Gervais. Write what you know."'

Settling on a different tactic, his next essay was about a neighbour and, to its writer, was 'the most boring thing in the world. When I got it back, Mr Taylor had written: "A, much better." Just then, a realization dawned: people want the truth. When I came to write *The Office* I remembered that.'

The influence of Mr Taylor lasted up to O level, when their paths diverged and Ricky followed his preferred science route at A level. But he believes his series of *Flanimals* books, illustrated volumes for children on imaginary creatures with bizarre names, combined both his old passion for science and his more recent love for language. 'But because of what I've ended up doing,' he acknowledged to the *TES*, 'it's Mr Taylor who was the teacher who made a difference to my life.'

When the opportunity had presented itself in 1979, he happily became one of six in his year to continue his education at university. 'I had this conviction that I was going to go,' he told the *TES*, 'so I knew I needed all eight O levels. Besides, I was a bit of a Lisa Simpson. I did the bare minimum work because I knew I'd pass anyway, but I wanted all the teachers to like me and know that if in doubt, no, it wasn't me who burned down the canteen.' Sure enough, having been told three C-grades at A level would be enough to secure his passport out of Reading, that is precisely what he achieved.

All those years of studying the flora and fauna of the back garden seemed to have paid off. His initial intention was to study biology – 'It seemed pointless to aim for anything other than something vocational,' said the next would-be David Attenborough – but within two weeks of arriving at University College London (UCL) he changed his course to philosophy when he realized how few lectures he would be obliged to attend for the latter subject. 'I thought, "Why am I still doing this? I didn't come here to study. This is *ridiculous*."'

The deciding factor seems to have been that the biology timetable featured two early lectures, which Ricky clearly didn't feel keen to attend. 'So I went along to the philosophy department and said, "I'm sorry, I've made a mistake. I wanted to do philosophy and I spelt it 'biology' by accident."'

Having wisely freed himself from the shackles of a labour-intensive course, the fresh-faced undergraduate from Reading now had plenty of extra time to devote to alternative pursuits, including those of a musical bent, which would see him embark on the next crucial stage in his quest for fame and fortune.

2

Philosophy and Pop

❝ I wanted to be a pop star, but I stopped when I realized I couldn't squeeze into the leather trousers. ❞

As HE SET OUT on the road to higher education, Ricky's family went on to live relatively normal lives. Brother Bob, a painter and decorator, and sister Marsha, a housewife, both stayed in the Reading area, while eldest sibling Larry put down roots further afield as a teacher in Glasgow. So when Eva and Jerry Gervais watched their youngest fledgling fly the nest in search of a degree, they little imagined that three years of study would turn out a pop star. And although his time in the spotlight was brief, it clearly gave him a taste for the stardom he'd take a decade and a half to achieve by other means.

If all you know of Ricky's musical ability is 'If You Don't Know Me By Now', David Brent's infamous party piece, or 'Lady Blue', his hideous ode to Marge Simpson, then his adventures as a bit-part player in the New Romantic era of the early 1980s may come as something of a surprise. The fact that, twenty years on, he nominated David Bowie for the title of Greatest Living Englishman ('though I'm loath to give it to a pop star') proves that some things haven't changed.

Later on, in the early 1990s, he'd briefly manage a nascent band by the name of Suede, whose singer Brett Anderson shared the Bowie fixation, giving Ricky the opportunity to live his dreams by proxy. First time around, though, the vehicle to take him to fame and fortune was Seona Dancing.

It was the era that spawned such well-loved twosomes as Soft Cell, the Pet Shop Boys and Blancmange, and it has to be said that Seona Dancing – pronounced Shaw-nuh – was, visually at least, in the running. While the man himself has always remained tight-lipped about this period of his life, a college friend of Ricky's has revealed that Seona Dancing was named after a girl who always looked to be particularly enjoying dancing at the UCL discos.

Ricky met fellow student William Moat in the university bar in June 1982, where, legend has it, their union was sealed by an impromptu performance of Sinatra's 'The Lady is a Tramp'. A swiftly compiled demo tape containing sixteen songs, the music composed by keyboard-player Bill (who, bizarrely, adopted the stage surname Macrae) to words written by his partner, won them a contract with London Records. RCA and CBS had also apparently shown interest. 'We were incredibly lucky to get a deal that way,' a grateful Macrae told *Smash Hits*, adding, 'the days are gone when you had to play pubs and clubs for five years before anybody noticed you.' Ricky's observations to the teen mag were simply to reveal his past experience as a choirboy and confess to being a Simon and Garfunkel fan. (Not that many teenage readers would have had a clue who the august 1960s folk-rockers actually were.)

According to the 1983 *Smash Hits Yearbook*, which daringly fingered the duo as one of 'Fifteen For Eighty-Four' alongside the great (Prince, Madonna), the good (Billy Bragg, Aztec Camera) and the now downright obscure (Phil Thornally, Naked Eyes), they then intriguingly 'vanished for a while into the obscurity of Brussels clubland, for reasons too complex to explain here'.

Seona Dancing's first single, which was released in May 1983, was 'More To Lose. Though high-tempo and danceable in a Human League-style way, it boasted the angsty chorus, 'And now it's over/Both of us free/And I feel colder.' The only person known to play the band on the radio in those days was Steve Wright on Radio 1 – and not more than a handful of times. The vocal over the drum machine and keyboards was, not surprisingly, very *Heroes*-era Bowie, while the B-side 'You're On My Side' was not dissimilar.

The duo, which Ricky's brother Bob witheringly described as 'some band with synthesizers and big hair', clearly failed to impress his closest family member. 'Ricky came to meet me once and he'd had extensions put in the back of his hair, like a mullet, for a photo shoot. It had cost him £92, which was a lot of money in 1982 [*sic*].' Bob took him to the building site where he was then working, with the intention of taking the mickey out of his brother. Somehow he persuaded a game Ricky to go up the side of a building in a cradle at the end of a crane jib. 'But he remained completely calm,' Bob admiringly recalled. 'Even when I rocked the cradle, swinging in mid-air, he was unfazed. The joke was on me that time.' That would be the highest a member of Seona Dancing ever ascended . . . everywhere except the Philippines, of which more anon.

Not daunted by their flop, the duo cut a follow-up – 'Bitter Heart', backed with 'Tell Her', released later in '83. The A-side once more majored on anguished lyrics – 'I'll end the angered cries and the twisted joys that rage in a bitter heart' – while the musical formula remained unchanged, with not a guitar or real drum in earshot. Yet again, though, in Ricky's words, 'It was in the Woolworths bargain bin practically before it was released.'

Joseph Watt, co-founder of bespoke San Francisco computer remixers Razormaids, somehow got hold of 'Bitter Heart' and stretched it out to a DJ-friendly six minutes seventeen seconds. Depeche Mode and Erasure were among others to enjoy such exclusive remix attention, so Seona Dancing's dynamic duo could have been excused for sitting back, rubbing their hands and anticipating a nice little earner to replace their now-exhausted student grants.

Fellow UCL student Sean Thomas was interested in getting a foothold in the world of journalism (he has since contributed to *The Times, Telegraph, Mail* and *Guardian,* as well as penning three novels). The combination of their ambitions resulted in the only known music-press interview with the duo appearing in trendsetting weekly *New Musical Express* in June 1983. The headline 'More To Lose, Everything To Gain' (punning the title of their first single) was accompanied by the sole press picture they seem to have posed for, which made Ricky and Bill look like two Andrew Ridgeleys (the guitar-miming 'other half' to George Michael in Wham!).

The majority of the words in a paper-thin half-page feature came from Thomas, with 'Ricky Gervaise [*sic*] . . . all eye teeth and languid voice', notably more talkative than his partner, portrayed as 'more anxious . . . continually flashing unnerving smiles'. The keyboardist had apparently selected Ricky as 'a face and a voice to match his own talents'.

When asked what differentiated Seona Dancing from their 'silicone siblings', Bill Macrae simply answered, 'We're better.' When the point was pressed, he decided they were 'trying to marry the rhythmic qualities of East Coast funk with the more melodic aspect of post-punk over here'. It's hard to tell from long-cold ink on page whether he was sending up his interviewer, his perceived audience or even himself with such an answer.

Given Seona Dancing's near-total lack of chart success – their singles reaching Numbers 116 and 70 respectively – there's an irony in Ricky's statement that, 'We've never consciously written songs with the chart in mind, thinking that this song is going to get to number so-and-so.' Not that he was ruling out the possibility. 'If they do chart it's very pleasing – it means many people have heard your record.' As for their image, 'If thirteen-year-olds want to buy our single because of our long eyelashes, then great.'

In the absence of any further vaguely sensible input from the duo, writer Thomas was obliged to flannel away, revealing that Ricky 'likes zippy philosopher and libertarian John Stuart Mill', desperately trying to justify the expenditure of *NME* newsprint space on a band clearly aimed at the teen *Smash Hits* market. They were also battling with the eternal conundrum of being Socialists who had been offered 'an unprecedentedly large percentage royalty for a new group'. Not that Ricky had ever been on the breadline as a student, having cheerfully got used to living within his means on £5 a day, courtesy of a full grant.

Quizzed as to his youthful pop ambitions by *The Observer* in 2005, Ricky was quick – too quick, perhaps – to laugh off the venture as 'nothing, really. Every bloke in the country with a funny haircut has had a record deal at one time or another, or done a demo. We got signed, released a single and it failed, and that was it. We thought we were Tears For Fears for a bit. You only start really taking the mickey out of yourself when you hit thirty and become thirteen stone. While you are twenty-two and still have a thirty-inch waist you can take yourself as seriously as you like.'

It may be the old rose-tinted spectacles syndrome, but few overviews of the era that mention the duo have anything but praise for them. New Wave-fixated website Everything2.com described Seona Dancing as 'comparable to Fiction Factory with a splash of Simple Minds, the occasional glimpse of It's Immaterial and a dash of early Talk Talk. It's standard New Romantic fun, and it's pleasantly surprising to find that it's not too bad at all. With "More To Lose", a slightly echoing piano begins a plaintive melody, soon joined by the standard octave-hopping synth bass, sadly uninspired drums and a hint of strings in the background, adding warm depths with chord overlays.

'"Bitter Heart" begins with a more synth bass, following much the same pattern; strings layer over the top and Gervais, sounding strangely similar to David Bowie, begins. It's not groundbreaking stuff: Bill Macrae's keyboards provide that classic New Wave sound, and even the overblown poetic angst of Gervais's lyrics only serve to place it perfectly in the 1980s, just one amongst a hundred other short-lived pop duos.'

At the time, Sean Thomas described Ricky's vocal abilities as 'lazy and languorous . . . although his singing occasionally descends into mannerism'. What price that sixteen-track demo tape now, we wonder? The man himself likened Seona Dancing to boy-girl duo 'Yazoo – me being Alison Moyet. We got a record deal and our first single got to Number 116, the follow-up made it to Number 70, and then we didn't have a deal any more. I do miss being able to use eyeliner freely . . .'

The songs' disappointing performances at home means that even today, the gap between Senser and Sepultura in the *Guinness Book of Hit Singles* remains to be filled. *The Rare Record Price Guide 2006*, published by anoraks' bible *Record Collector*, however, values both seven-inch versions at £18, with their more plentiful extended twelve-inch counterparts at £10 and £12 respectively. All must possess the obligatory picture sleeve. Pirate copies of the twelve-inchers are regularly to be found on Internet auction sites and sell around the £30 mark, this princely sum securing a 'white label' copy plus a photo of the men responsible or a colour photocopy of the equally embarrassing sleeve.

The band's unexpected peak of popularity in the Philippines came in 1985 and was not of their making, but a clever ruse by a pop radio station in Manila. The station, call-sign DWRT FM, started giving the song heavy airplay under a false song title and artist name so that their competitors wouldn't be able to find the record and play it themselves. A station ID jingle was even inserted midway through the track, making it impossible for other DJs to play a recording on their own stations. The popularity of song and station soared.

It took a full year for the identity of the song, previously announced as 'Fade' by Medium, to be revealed. By that time, 'More To Lose' had become, in the breathless words of Michael Sutton of *All Music Guide*, 'the theme song of angst-ridden New Wave youths in the Philippines . . . With its brooding, Michael Hutchence-like vocals and jumpy percussion, it swept the clubs.' Of course, it was all too late for Seona Dancing, who had broken up in 1984 when their contract with London Records was not extended. Those two singles would remain their epitaph. As for Bill Moat/Macrae, little is known about his subsequent activities, except for the fact that he worked in a record shop in the late 1980s.

An interesting sidelight was thrown on these days in November 2002, when Sean Thomas, the man responsible for the *NME* feature in 1983, wrote a piece for *The Times* reflecting on his former friend's rise to fame and contrasting it with another, Gavin Rossdale of guitar band Bush. (Rossdale's fame has, ironically, since been eclipsed by that of blonde bombshell wife Gwen Stefani.) The sub-editor's introduction set the scene: 'When an old friend suddenly becomes famous and successful it can seem exciting. But then other emotions stir, such as jealousy and envy. Our correspondent explains his feelings about his celebrity chums . . .'

Thomas then took up the story. 'In the early 1980s Ricky was reading English [*sic*] at University College London. I was doing philosophy. Ricky was a wannabe star (he was trying to become a pop star), and I was a wannabe writer. As we drank in the same student bars, it seemed perfect that I should write a profile of his band for the *New Musical Express*. The band failed, through no fault of Ricky's. Yes, he was a tad vain, yes, he wore diamanté earrings, but he was a good singer, and the single was above average.

'In time we moved on and diverged. A couple of years later I bumped into him and it seemed that he had lost a bit of his bumptiousness. After that I didn't see him for fifteen years. Then a couple of years ago he appeared on TV as a comedian. I was stunned. Here was gifted-but-unlucky, funny-but-failed Ricky being famous. Admittedly he was chubbier than the cheekboned New Romantic I remembered – but there was no denying it. He had made it . . .'

Thomas and Gervais ran into each other again, sparking the idea for the article, on Ricky's home turf – the British Museum in Bloomsbury. 'I saw Ricky strolling past the information counter. "Hi," I said. "Remember me?" Ricky stopped, smiled, and said "Of course" and was deftly charming. We talked about his band and the ancient *NME* interview. Then we shook hands, promised each other a drink, and went our separate ways. It was only as I emerged into the frost of a Bloomsbury evening that I realized he probably hadn't recalled my name. Ha!'

Seona Dancing's brief, two-single legacy would go on to rear its head in several unexpected contexts. Invited to TV's *Room 101* to consign several of his pet hates to history, an unsuspecting Ricky was ambushed by the video clip for 'More To Lose', which was set in a blacksmith's. Bill Moat was smiting metal while angel-faced Ricky delivered the lines to camera. As he squirmed in the chair, it was clear that this was a ghost from the past that would never be completely laid to rest.

He was asked about it again in an interview with *The Observer* in 2001. 'Loosely, it was an electronic duo boy band, Tears For Fears, that sort of thing,' he explained. 'We got signed on a demo tape, released a couple of singles, they didn't do anything, and the record company went, "Cheers, lads, keep the money, don't bother us again."'

And then it happened again when Coldplay's Chris Martin, with whom Ricky co-starred in a January 2006 *Q* magazine feature entitled 'Attack of the Clowns', turned on him. 'What about that band you were in? Antigone Rising? Saracen's Haircut?' mocked his fellow UCL graduate. Ricky, unnerved, swiftly changed the subject . . . to cult rock spoof film *This is Spinal Tap*.

Ricky's encounter with the Rob Reiner film was, in retrospect, the most significant music-related experience to happen to him in 1983. 'It was a big thing for me,' he confirmed many years later. 'When I first saw *This Is Spinal Tap*, I immediately watched it again. I can't remember a film I've done that with, before or since. To get so deep into the genre that they were spoofing, the details of human behaviour, and then to do it all in someone else's native accent just blew me away. There's just a few things that go to comedy heaven – *Spinal Tap*, Laurel and Hardy, *The Simpsons,* and Derek and Clive.'

He saw many echoes of Seona Dancing in *Spinal Tap*, even if heavy metal and electro-pop were stylistically poles apart. 'It's bad that I was in a band like Spinal Tap and really meant it,' he'd conclude, 'but it's good that I realized that before it was too late. It's like someone coming up to me and saying, "My friends say that I'm like David Brent." That's just bad. It's bad that you are and it's bad that you like it.'

If pop stardom was not to be an option, it was just as well Ricky departed the groves of academe with a respectable qualification – a 2:1 degree in philosophy. Something else he left university with was long-term partner Jane Fallon. His meeting her turned out to be far more significant than his acquaintance with Bill Moat/ Macrae, but it happened in the self-same students' union bar in 1982.

'He was very thin, tiny,' said Jane to the *Daily Mirror*, in one of her rare interviews, in 2002. 'He had one of those long, floppy, New Romantic fringes over one eye and wore loads of floppy shirts. My main memory of that time, though, is that the bar was grotty and smelled of old sandwiches and stale beer. Maybe that's what started Ricky's passion for cheese sandwiches! We were there with mutual friends and it went from there. We got on really well and really clicked. There wasn't a lightning bolt moment, but he made me laugh.'

Interviewer Ryan Parry suggested it was this shared sense of humour that represented the glue that had held their relationship together for so long. Certainly, it seemed to be a case of opposites attracting. Ricky was, at that time, sharing a typical student flat in Finsbury Park, north London, with a number of other similarly slobby students, compared with which Jane's room in the university halls of residence was cleanliness itself.

Finsbury Park was far-flung by Ricky's standards. He had at one point lived in a London University-owned student house in Taviton Street, which may yet be a candidate for a commemorative 'blue plaque' in the future. He clearly enjoyed the Bloomsbury experience, for it is here that he still makes his home today.

Final-year student Jane had, like Ricky, changed her course (from law to history) because the former had seemed too much like hard work. 'We had our laziness in common, I suppose. We rarely went to lectures and preferred lazing in bed. We weren't great joiners-in . . . We spent most of our time asleep.' Surprisingly, perhaps, Ricky graduated with a better class of degree than his girlfriend.

When the pair finally moved in together, they managed to run to a grotty flat above a sauna. She remembers: 'It was a stinky, horrible little bedsit with one room and a kitchen, and we had to share a toilet with neighbours. But we had a laugh and we were happy being together.'

Jane soon discovered who had been responsible for the overflowing sink of dirty dishes she'd grown to hate at Finsbury Park. Life together was described as 'very messy', with 'cheese all over the floor and crumbs all over the sofa. He leaves everything everywhere while I'm quite tidy. He also makes a lot of noise, he is constantly singing stupid songs and squeaking and making funny noises . . .' No change there, then.

She also recalled the time when his student grant had been spent and the hot water had just run out. Ricky put his last 50p piece in the meter, emptied a packet of washing powder into the bath, threw in his filthy clothes, then jumped in after them. 'I know, it sounds a little strange – but that's Ricky. He's always unpredictable,' shrugged Jane.

Having returned to the Bloomsbury area and settled down, Ricky was loath to relocate further afield and certainly was not prepared to return to Reading. 'I didn't have any money growing up and it was fine,' he's said of his university years. 'I had a full grant there and felt very rich with my fiver a day. The leanest years were after college, on the dole and stuff.' But, consistent with his working-class origins, he was rarely, if ever, overdrawn. 'I think I had nowt for a long time, but no debts.' When it came to money, resources were pooled, 'But Jane is the most organized at paying household bills.'

After a spell as a cleaner at the university and helping to run security for student gigs, Ricky eventually found more permanent employment when he took a full-time job as entertainments officer for the University of London Students' Union (ULU).

'It was a nice job,' he explains, 'but I was twice as old as the people I was telling what to dance to. I had visions of programming a Belgian jungle [music] night at fifty-five: "Come on, it's all the rage."' He'd later add, 'It was like being the prime minister . . . mildly embarrassing, really.' Ricky worked at the Union for several years, in which time he developed the idea that was to launch him to stardom.

Fellow union worker Julie Adams, then a finance manager, recalls Gervais as 'very good at mimicking other people we worked with. I know there are a few characters in *The Office* that are based on our office in the Students' Union, but I'm keeping my lips sealed as to who.' The entertainments officer was very entertaining in himself, and could create mayhem among his workmates when the mood took him – especially when alcohol was added to the mix to encourage him to leave his workaday self behind. 'We'd go out for a drink after work,' said Julie, 'and he would have us in stitches.'

As partner Jane was already making waves in the world of television, the double income allowing them to afford the not inconsiderable rent of their central London flat, Ricky could have been excused for feeling that he was underachieving. But when an *Observer* journalist quizzed him about this after his rise to fame, he denied there had been any sense of failure. 'When I was working at ULU I never thought, "This is shit," or, "The money is bad." I thought, "This is quite a good job." I suppose if all this had not come along I might now have been a forty-three-year-old entertainments manager. But that never worried me at the time.'

In many ways, his ULU role was setting him up for writing *The Office*. But it also gave him the chance to rub shoulders with budding music stars. He tried his hand at management with a number of bands, admitting as much to *Q* in January 2004: 'I used to manage a Queen tribute band called Closet Queens. They were going to call themselves Right Fred's Dead, but that's just a bit sick . . .'

That band, who had started life as (the singular) Closet Queen before renaming themselves Killer Queen after the original band's 1974 Top Three hit, had actually formed a year after Freddie Mercury's death in November 1991. This made them not only among the first Queen tribute acts, but one of the first tribute bands overall. Made up of a group of students, they were led by one Pat

Myers, who still fronts them to this day. Their first full show at the University of London Union was at the annual Freshers' Ball, quite a prestigious event for a new band. It had been preceded by an 'in-store' appearance at Tower Records and a show at a student hall of residence.

Brennan Young was employed as the band's 'fifth member', filling in on keyboards when Myers was camping it up centre stage in full Mercury effect. In an interview with Elliott Day's informative *Office* website (www.wernhamhogg.co.uk), Young remembered Ricky calling the prestigious Marquee Club in Wardour Street, Soho, and using 'the manner of David Brent when hiring the forklift driver' to procure them a gig.

Although Gervais had yet to see them live, this trivial detail certainly didn't stop him from laying it on thick. 'Ricky got on the telephone and called the Marquee and said, "I've just seen this band. They're amazing, a Queen cover band and it's just like a bloody video. You won't believe it. If you hear from them you've got to get them on." All this hyperbole. When he'd finished, he pushed the phone across the desk to Pat. Pat called the Marquee and said, "Hi, it's Pat from Closet Queen." They said, "Oh, we've heard about you, do you want to do a gig?"'

Gervais's tasks as band manager, which he carried out to the satisfaction of all, included arranging concert dates, organizing a van and securing the services of reliable roadies. He also knew who to call to ensure gig listings were accompanied by a photograph to give them prominence on the page. Brennan Young recalled 'an interview for some university rag mag where the student journalist asked what it was like to be the biggest cover band out or something. At that point we had still only done a handful of gigs! After the interviewers left the dressing room, Pat and Ricky couldn't contain their amazement or their glee. Of course, Ricky had primed them in advance somehow, like he did with the Marquee gig.'

'Everyone with half a brain knows that pop culture is driven by hype and illusions like that,' Young continued, 'but it's quite astonishing to see it happen under your nose, and to meet someone who can pull the strings so deftly. Ricky seemed incredibly aware of all the machinations which make a band popular, and he was well connected; working as ents manager for ULU he got to meet everybody. That was a great thing for Closet (Killer) Queen in those days. Our third gig was in front of 3,000 people! That's pretty astonishing, and only Ricky could have made it happen.'

Interestingly, the band had a Welsh bassist called Gareth playing the role of Queen quiet-man John Deacon, who was 'extremely aloof and serious, and used to say and do the most outrageous "foot-in-mouth" things'. Brennan Young is certain that his namesake in *The Office* was partly based on him. It's also amusing to learn that there was talk of Ricky dressing up as David Bowie to take a cameo role when the band performed 'Under Pressure', the 1981 chart-topper that saw Bowie and Queen join forces, which was a highlight of Killer Queen's stage act. That suggestion, though it never actually happened, was, in Young's view, 'a typical example of what I remember as Ricky's blurring of megalomaniac fantasy and deadpan humour'.

Brennan Young concluded: 'Ricky is fascinated by vanity and narcissism. Fame, especially pop culture fame, is a kind of shamanistic narcissism. We all want to be movie stars or pop stars or comedians, and it's an impossible dream for most of us, so we continue to worship these weird "medicine men" who go on stage with funny clothes and perform. All those *Fame Academy* type programmes leverage that fantasy, as does *The Office*, viz., Michael Jackson impressions, guitar-playing during seminars, "comedy" in the workplace, etc. The core contradiction is that "it could be me in that spotlight", but for ninety-nine per cent of the audience who harbour that desire, it's never going to happen, no matter how talented they might be.

'What's interesting is that Ricky has become a star himself by exploiting that same fantasy world in the head of one of his characters. That's what I meant when I said Ricky is very much like David Brent – Ricky is probably just as vain as David Brent. The difference is that Ricky also finds it grotesque and hilarious, so when you see Ricky on *Parkinson* or whatever, there are always these unbelievable gambits of false modesty, and the deadpan delivery just carries it. Ricky wears his narcissism on his sleeve, like a trail of snot. It's very punk, actually.'

Another band Ricky was involved with in a loosely managerial capacity was Suede. Based around sometime students Brett Anderson and Justine Frischmann, they were at first a hard sell, even after Justine (who went off to form her own band, Elastica) was replaced by Bernard Butler. In the words of *Q*'s Dave Cavanagh, 'Suede gigs throughout 1990 and 1991 were a mixture of catcall cacophonies and silence, as audiences tried to get their collective heads round a bunch of mincing glam prima donnas in crimplene fronted by a seriously overdoing-it limp-wrist [Anderson] warbling untold perversions in music-hall Cockney.' Two singles later they were the potential band of 1993. By that time, of course, their path and that of Ricky Gervais had diverged.

When quizzed by David Pollock of *The Scotsman* a decade and a half after their liaison, guitarist Butler laughingly admitted that Gervais had been involved in their early days, 'And he was f**king rubbish! There was nothing funny about him managing us, let me tell you. Around 1990 he was the ents manager at the University of London Union, and they used to have this big open-plan office, which is probably where he got the idea for *The Office.* I actually didn't notice he had a sense of humour at the time.'

Fascinatingly, Butler also suggests that Gervais had yet to abandon his own long-held dreams of musical fame. 'He was trying to be a pop star himself with a band called Son of Bleeper, and we'd support them because it was the only way we could get a gig. Supporting Ricky Gervais and his crap band!' At this memory, the former Suede guitarist dissolved into laughter. 'To be fair, we were bloody useless as well. It was absolutely the best thing for both of us that we went our separate ways.' (All efforts by the author to trace any details about Son of Bleeper have proved fruitless.)

In 2002, talking to *The Daily Telegraph,* Ricky agreed to differ on the subject of Suede's potential: 'They were good. I was rubbish.' But he would never disown his dream entirely, claiming that *The Office* sub-text of unful-filled potential came to mind during his ents manager days. 'We all do [regular jobs]. I did them for years and I'll probably do them again and there's nothing whatsoever wrong with that. This is more about people saying, "That's it, then. I'm sixty, I've lived in Slough, I've had this job – and all the time I wanted to be a drummer."

'It's the tragedy of the failure of the dream: we can't all be pop stars and we can't all be astronauts . . . That doesn't mean that an office job is necessarily wasting your life. It means that if it's not right for you and you know it then don't kid yourself. Some people just hang on in there.' Sadly for Ricky, he was beaten to pop stardom by fellow UCL graduates Chris Martin (Greek and Latin, 1999), Will Champion (anthropology, 1999) and Jonny Buckland (mathematics, 1999) – the fourth member of Coldplay having quit mid-course.

Nowadays, Gervais gets his musical kicks from various wannabe-pop-star talent shows: 'Especially the first few rounds when there are contestants bordering on the mentally ill . . . It gets exciting again when it gets to the last ten.' That, and the fact he thinks Simon Cowell is 'a really nice bloke'. There's no accounting for taste.

Student politics, or entertainment directed at the politically aware, was not Ricky's thing, and exposure to it certainly helped shape his own entertainment ambitions. As he explained to *The Observer*, he was not about to follow in the footsteps of Ben Elton and become a stand-up political satirist. 'If a comedian tells me that sometimes politicians are corrupt or dictators are bad, my reaction will be, No shit, never thought of that before. I have no interest in telling people that George W. [Bush] is not all he might be. For that reason my comedy targets tend to be, you know, Gandhi or Thora Hird.'

The alternative comedy scene flourishing in the 1980s and epitomized by the likes of *The Young Ones* and Alexei

Sayle was, in his view, 'A little too linked to fixed themes. It was a cause more than a comedy movement – a reaction to Bernard Manning.'

So Ricky got his head down, and as well as revelling in the more interesting aspects of his job, such as selecting and booking bands, he also spent time involved in the more mundane side of things 'working in a normal environment, taking mental notes . . . I've been through the whole office existence – management training courses, role plays, away days, staff assessments.' He even decided to build a wall of files around his workspace 'to get my own office as I didn't like open-plan'. He would occasionally emerge from this hideaway 'to do a lot of walking around with a piece of paper on the way to the photocopier'.

Ricky had seemed likely to remain an entertainments manager for the foreseeable future, but that prospect didn't appear to worry him. 'I always thought something will turn up,' he recalled – and so it did when he was approached by nascent London radio station Xfm (whose offices were handily placed in nearby Charlotte Street) to help them with a publicity campaign aimed at his student constituency.

Officially launched in September 1997, Xfm had been intended as a local radio station, broadcasting to the capital's fans of alternative music. Many, of course, would be students. With bands previously regarded as alternative, like Oasis and Blur, having crossed over to the 'mainstream' charts in the previous couple of years, it was certainly a timely move.

And it also gave Ricky, whose assistance with their student PR drive impressed them enough to offer him the job of 'Head of Speech', a great opportunity to further his career. For Xfm is where he started to turn his observations of years spent in that open-plan office into a wickedly funny TV show. Despite the grand title, the job – which gave Ricky responsibility for all the speech output, such as the news and competitions – was bordering on the clerical. Notwithstanding his office experience, however, he didn't really know much about what he was supposed to do, as he himself later admitted. He managed to convince his bosses that the workload was too heavy for one person, and that he required some help. Thus he met and hired Stephen Merchant, a recent graduate with all-important radio experience. 'He [Ricky] got the job and had never worked in radio before,' explained 'Assistant to the Head of Speech' Merchant. 'He needed an assistant and my CV was on the top of the pile.'

To say Merchant, Gervais's partner in crime to this day, was unimpressed by his new boss on their first meeting would be an understatement. 'Ricky was meant to supervise all the speech output on the station, which was ridiculous. Have you heard him speak?' But Ricky was not prepared to stay behind the scenes. He saw himself behind the microphone, and his first impact on the airwaves came in the shape of contributions to ex-Radio 1 presenter Claire Sturgess's show. It required a certain amount of balls to sail into the breach, and Gervais rates it his most nervous moment until auditioning for the animated film *Valiant* in 2005. 'I remember thinking, I'm going to embarrass myself here,' he recalls.

An evening talk show of his own proved short-lived, but suggested he was already an expert at self-deprecation. In a later interview, he'd admit to being 'no

John Peel' but laid into the 'personality jocks' whom he declined to name individually. 'I can't stand the arrogance of DJs who think anything they say will be interesting. Why broadcast if you've nothing to say? It's easy doing the radio because if you run out of words you just go: "Here's Radiohead!"'

Working in radio gave Ricky the chance to emulate one of his entertainment idols, Kenny Everett. Producer David Mallet described Everett, who worked on Capital and Radio 1 in the 1970s before proceeding to the small screen, as 'not a comedian, but had an innate sense of comedy'. It's a description Ricky himself would be proud to bear.

Gervais and Merchant were eventually given their own show on a Sunday evening, but even on an alternative music station they were determined to push what boundaries there were. One oft-repeated story had them daring to play 'Man Don't Give A F**k', a song by Welsh band Super Furry Animals. With more than fifty swear words in the lyrics, intoned over a Steely Dan sample, it required adept use of the fader to make it broadcastable. The daring duo attempted to make a random noise in place of each of the fifty-plus f**ks, but Gervais failed and swore in frustration . . . Very Everett!

Xfm's own history would prove a chequered one. It had developed from Q102, a pirate station that turned 'legit' as the 1980s turned to the 1990s and launched at least one career in the shape of DJ Steve Lamacq. After broadcasts under a restricted service licence had proved there was a market for its music, it launched on a permanent basis on 1 September 1997. But the death of Princess Diana the day before stole the headlines, and

Xfm arguably never recovered. (A delay in launch was impossible due to a series of gigs that had been planned to coincide.)

Its marketing campaign was weak, and in May the following year Xfm was taken over by the GCap Media Group that owned Capital Radio, gung-ho on the acquisitions front after having their bid for Virgin rejected by Chris Evans. (Ironically, Xfm would be Evans's next stop after leaving Virgin under a cloud in June 2001.)

With hindsight, Xfm was on a hiding to nothing even before Diana's death. With self-deprecating slogans like 'Nine out of ten people said they preferred Capital' and 'If other stations are middle of the road, we're lying drunk in a ditch,' its listenership hovered under 250,000 – half the hoped- and budgeted-for figure. Ricky's student background had clearly helped him blag the job, but he had boarded a ship that, if not sinking, was listing markedly.

Xfm relaunched on 28 August 1998 with a tightly formatted playlist of US-style modern rock, not unlike that of the nationally available Virgin. Specialist shows were axed, and even the recruitment of ex-Boomtown Rat/Live Aid svengali Bob Geldof for a drivetime show (which he later confessed to *The Guardian* he hated) couldn't restore credibility.

The original, if small, band of Xfm listeners was not happy about the inevitable broadening of format, and figures plummeted to below 200,000. There were 500-strong public protests outside Capital's offices in Leicester Square on 10 October, and Ricky loudly participated. Inevitably, it ended with him being made redundant. 'They asked what I did and I said, "Well, muck around, sort of. Can you keep on paying me?" They said no. I wouldn't have survived the change because it wasn't my thing. Radio work was quite a fun way to make a living; I just liked playing records. It was better than trying to be David Bowie for years.'

Just after he was made redundant, Ricky compered a gig by indie hopefuls The Samurai Seven, organized in Camden to protest at Capital's high-handed approach. As with most of his actions in this period, this has been airbrushed from his official biography since, after his rise to fame, his former employers made every effort possible to persuade him to return – and succeeded!

Back in 1998, the Radio Authority received a record 600 complaints about Xfm's repositioning and responded by fining Capital £5,000 – a small gnat-bite in terms of their extensive resources. Such names as Zoë Ball and Dermot O'Leary were later drafted in, and listening figures were eventually hiked up at the expense of the original blueprint – though, to be fair, specialist programming in the evenings has since gone some way to fulfilling the original remit. Sister stations in Manchester and Scotland have established the Xfm brand, and with Ricky back in the fold they have a highly marketable face to use in their advertising.

Among the listeners to the 'original' Xfm were Coldplay, with whom Ricky had plenty in common: they'd formed at University College London not long after Gervais vacated his post as entertainments manager to join Xfm. When they met up years later, Ricky admitted he'd been given their first demo tape at the radio station . . . and lost it! 'We certainly didn't hear it on your show,' remarked singer Chris Martin, who said the band used to tune in to Xfm every week in the hope they would win the Demo Clash competition. Perhaps that's why they never did . . .

Working at Xfm had provided Ricky with his first opportunity for public family wind-ups. And though the station's transmission range didn't extend as far as Reading, his mother was well aware of his style. 'Mum didn't like him swearing on the radio,' remembers brother Bob. 'So one day he phoned her on air. Only she didn't realize, and he broadcast her saying, "Don't bloody swear so much on the radio."' Eva's horror only increased when Ricky later progressed to working on *The 11 O'Clock Show*, a Channel 4 comedy show more talked about than watched.

According to legend, Gervais had spent some of his working hours, in the calm before the Capital takeover, amusing his co-workers with a comic character he called 'Seedy Boss'. And Stephen Merchant was impressed enough to remember it when he decided to move into television. With what Merchant calculated was twelve years' office experience between the pair – 'I used to temp and do really tedious stuff like filing and stuffing envelopes' – he was keen to capture 'the monotony, the constant squabbling'.

The stage was set for a classic collaboration.

3

Partner in Crime

❝ *He's eight foot tall, has stupid glasses, awful hair,
but it makes me look good . . . I want people to know
that he is a freak and I'm the normal one.* ❞

IF RICKY GERVAIS is indeed, as John Humphrys was
informed, 'possibly the biggest name on TV these
days', then the name of Stephen Merchant, his co-writer
in every entertainment project in which he's been
involved to date, should surely be considerably better
known than it is. He is the McCartney to Gervais's
Lennon, the less public half of the double act that has
produced TV gold.

Merchant grew up in Bristol, a city umbilically
connected to Gervais's Reading via the M4 motorway. It
was he who suggested actor Mackenzie Crook play the
part of Gareth in a West Country accent 'because we
think there's nothing funnier than [a West Countryman]
trying to be taken seriously'. It's also led to people tuning

in to the Gervais/Merchant double act on radio and erroneously assuming Crook, a Londoner in real life, to be Ricky's straight man.

Born on 24 November 1974, the eldest child of plumber Ron and Elaine, a nursery nurse, Stephen Merchant was brought up in Hanham, a middle-class suburb a fair way from Bristol city centre. His biggest problem at school was bearing the jibes about his excessive height: he only stopped growing at six feet seven inches. In all, however, memories of his schooldays at Hanham High are generally as positive as were Ricky's in Reading. 'I always had a good time; it wasn't particularly rough. It was a good experience.'

Unlike his future partner, his school was co-educational, yet he was particularly shy in addressing the opposite sex, again possibly a by-product of his height. He also suffered terribly from hay fever, which made summers something of a red-nosed nightmare, and reportedly has a weak bladder. (The combination of these two health matters has led to the ill-informed erroneously grouping him with those celebs who visit the toilet more regularly than most for 'recreational' purposes.)

The jokes about his height have persisted, and if Merchant has one wish, now he has found some measure of fame, it would be that 'people looked and thought, "Oh, there's that bloke who did those TV programmes," as opposed to, "What a freaky weirdo . . ." It's amazing how people feel they can make fun of your height when they never would if you were fat or disabled.'

His family are much closer to him in age than Ricky's, and have warmed to his work. Indeed, his sister, Alex, four years his junior, worked as art director on *The Office*, while dad Ron made a cameo appearance as Gordon, a handyman fascinated by the camera. In real life, his father has since given up plumbing in favour of working in community service supervision – a career Elaine now also follows.

The young Merchant was very much into drama, which he would go on to study at A level, and, like Ricky, he was a perennial star of school plays. One performance in particular, a comedy vicar, drew acclaim from all those who witnessed it. He's been since asked back to address current Hanham High pupils as the old boy who helped give the world *The Office*. Though he admits he doesn't revisit his old haunts a great deal because of pressure of work, the lure of family life tempts the bachelor back for an annual Yuletide pilgrimage: 'I always come back for Christmas and love to see all my old mates.'

Having achieved three A grades (his other subjects being English and history) at A level, Stephen went up to Warwick University and spent the early 1990s reading film and literature.

During the academic holidays he took various jobs, the most memorable of which was working in the admin department at Kleeneze, the well-known door-to-door sales firm ('Want to earn £50 to £200 a week? In five minutes, we will show you how!') not far from the family home. His job there was to log in damaged goods customers had returned. More rewardingly, he did some work experience at the *Bristol Evening Post* and wrote 'on and off' for *Venue*, the local weekly listings magazine for Bristol and Bath.

His broadcasting experience had begun as a film reviewer on the student radio station Radio Warwick.

Indeed, the station's 1995–6 yearbook presciently tipped him for great things, dubbing him, 'The man behind the funniest show on W963, the "Steve Show", highlights of which included an inspired take-off of the IRN news ("We spoke to Gerry Adams . . ."), an advert for Coventry Library ("Coventry Library makes no claims to be infinite"), attempting to give away an Aerosmith video to people on the toilet in Rootes [hall of residence], telephoning the library bridge security post to ask if they had seen a lost ball, as well as a series of snippets entitled "At home with Rose and Fred West". This show stood out from the crowd, as it was actually genuinely good. It's only a matter of time before Steve and his posse follow in the footsteps of Newman and Baddiel.'

Real life doesn't happen quite that smoothly, and, when a career path didn't immediately present itself on graduation, Stephen returned to Bristol to pick up the threads of his former life. Among the dead-end office jobs that would provide valuable inspiration for the future was a call centre, which he has compared to being 'like a Korean sweat-shop'. 'We answered the phone with set phrases,' he told the *Sunday Express*. 'It was very Stalinist. Two guys were fired for playing battleships between calls. I was reprimanded for not filling the requisite number of envelopes in the allotted time. I found the whole atmosphere so dispiriting.' He only lasted three days there because 'it was too intense'.

An ambition to become a stand-up comic, inspired by cross-dressing Eddie Izzard, then at the height of his cutting-edge popularity, was a potential way out. Merchant tested the water at the city's Comedy Box, the venue launched in 1994 where Graham Norton played his first ever stand-up gig and where the stage had been graced by the likes of Peter Kay, Al (Pub Landlord) Murray and Bill Bailey. It would prove a reality check for the young Bristolian. 'The first week I did well,' he remembers. 'Then the second week I died on my arse. I realized that stand-up was not that easy after all.' Nevertheless, his CV records the fact that he was a finalist in the 1998 *Daily Telegraph* Open Mic Comedy Awards.

A year after graduation, Stephen applied to the newly formed Xfm for a job as Ricky Gervais's assistant. His broadcast experience until then had included some work for Radio Bristol, and then a spell with the one-time pirate radio station Radio Caroline. This had attempted to relaunch as a local radio station for Bristol, but one-month trial stints in 1996 and 1997 failed to result in anything more permanent.

In an attempt to recapture the buccaneering North Sea pirate spirit, broadcasting took place from the *Thekla*, a coaster about two-thirds the size of the original *Ross Revenge*, which was converted into a floating theatre by Viv Stanshall of Bonzo Dog Doo-Dah Band fame. The singer and raconteur had sailed it 732 nautical miles from its former home in Sunderland to Bristol's city-centre docks and, with second wife Ki Longfellow-Stanshall, he had converted it into the Old Profanity Showboat. After Stanshall's accidental death in 1995, the vessel had been successfully used as a floating nightclub. With stick and string equipment, and flying by the seat of their pants, the relaunched Caroline managed to be heard up to thirty miles away.

Merchant had, by his own admission, come to music late in his adolescent life. 'My parents only had *Geoff Love and His Orchestra Play Big War Themes,* so I had to discover it for myself. For some reason, I felt that my parents would be appalled if I listened to music, and I remember secretly listening to Radio 2. How rock'n'roll can *that* be?' His first musical hero was Smiths frontman Morrissey, who Gervais (some thirteen years his senior) claims was 'a geek'. Merchant, for his part, admits he 'loved The Smiths, although I don't think they were as influential as, say, Black Sabbath or Nirvana'.

The station's musical remit was similar to that of Xfm, but with a slight but significant nod to the past: they not only played indie favourites, but also older acts that had exerted an influence on them. 'By adopting this music policy,' it claimed, Caroline was 'going back to what it was doing in the 1960s, i.e. playing music that no one else was. In a bold move we also decided not to play "Caroline" by the Fortunes as a station theme on the grounds that it's crap, and that it would alienate anyone under the age of sixty or anyone with any musical taste.'

Merchant appeared as half of Steve and Dan, a pairing who preferred to broadcast without surnames. Over to the Caroline website for further details: 'Steve, a ridiculously tall six foot seven, is also a stand-up comedian. Dan prefers to tell jokes sitting down. Their show proved so popular that they were awarded the prestigious breakfast slot for the second Bristol broadcast, although at one point their show was considered too good and they were sacked live on air . . . Steve once appeared as a contestant on *Blockbusters*. He lost.'

Somebody else on the early-morning scene at that time was Emma Boughton, who'd followed a similar course to Stephen: 'I started off doing student radio at university and then I did Radio Caroline when it docked in Bristol and did a few breakfast shows.' She then got a job at Creation Records and, thanks to career guidance from ex-DJ turned talent spotter Mark Goodier, found herself on Radio 1 in April 1998. Emma B, as she is professionally known, is now a broadcaster with London's Heart 106.2.

When Radio Caroline was offered a third chance in 2004, quaintly named station manager Steve Satan (amazingly not a Gervais/Merchant invention) was keen to use their most successful recent graduates as a selling point. 'Last time we had Stephen and also Emma B, who's gone on to work at Radio 1. We are hoping we can find someone who will be as famous again this time!' (The fate of Dan, the other half of Stephen's breakfast double act, is not known.)

For Stephen Merchant, as he surveyed the job market in 1997, his brief brush with fame had at least left him with a tape or two of his broadcasts, not to mention the ambition to break into radio. The next move was to send a cassette to a radio station he had read about in the *New Musical Express*. 'The person who opened my letter and listened to my tape was Ricky, who hired me as his assistant.' It was to prove a mutually beneficial partnership for, as Merchant reveals, his new boss candidly told him he'd 'no idea about radio whatsoever'.

Oh, to have been a fly on the wall at the interview that preceded Merchant's hiring. 'I said, "I don't know what I'm doing, but if you do all the work you can get away with murder,"' says Gervais, who insists that, at the time, Merchant's ambition was still to become a stand-up comic. Explaining his initial impressions of the situation to *The Independent on Sunday*'s Sholto Byrnes, Merchant recalled: 'As soon as I got there I realized he really didn't know what he was doing and was probably going to get us both fired.'

It is perhaps a tribute to their rapport that such an equal partnership should have developed, despite the thirteen-year age gap. 'We'll continue as long as we still enjoy it,' Merchant said of their partnership in 2005, adding, 'It's a bit like a marriage. We bring different things to the table, although I'm not sure what they are.' *The Office* producer Ash Atalla claims to have rarely seen any difference of opinion between them: 'They had a deal on *The Office* where if one person had a doubt and couldn't be talked out of it, then it didn't happen.'

Back in 1997, while he was delighted to be hired, Merchant had little doubt that the situation he found himself in was unlikely to last. 'I mean, I went up to London thinking he was like a big media hot-shot, and I turn up and he's wearing sweat-pants and a vest, or something, and clearly didn't know what he was doing. [He was] officially my boss, but it was ludicrous.'

There was even greater cause for concern because Merchant had committed himself to living in the capital, having put down a deposit and rented a place to live in Brixton. Curiously, he had only heard of the south London suburb in relation to the race riots of the 1980s, and would later move to nearby Kennington, but left there after 'one too many shootings' nearby. 'There was one outside our local burger shop,' he says. 'They were crap burgers, but . . .'

Merchant has since bought a flat in north London where he lives on his own. He chose it, he says, because it is close to the cinema and the supermarket, thus catering to his two most urgent needs. Back in 1997, though, his most urgent need was a stable job. 'It was going to cost me money if I had to go all the way back to Bristol . . . I was really worried.'

Little wonder, then, that he opted to quit the chaotic Xfm for the solidity of a traineeship with the BBC. (Both Merchant and Gervais have been inconsistent regarding the length of Merchant's employment at Xfm, the time period preceding his departure ranging between a week and three months depending on who is telling the story.) Although it seemed as if the partnership would fizzle out when he left the station for pastures new, it became apparent that a deeper, lasting connection had clearly already been made, and their paths would soon cross again.

The brief spell at Xfm was obviously fun. Merchant recalls mischief revolving around promotional samples that they would be given. 'Somebody came in with a balloon filled with Rice Krispies, which I put above my desk,' he recalled to Bruce Dessau. 'So one day I'm doing some filing or some work and Ricky was rolling around on his chair (which had wheels, and it was a polished floor). So I'm working trying to keep both our heads above water, I hear a pop, and he's just *covered* in Rice Krispies . . .'

At this point, Gervais was cracking up – the more so because Merchant, in the parental role despite their age difference, was insisting it was Gervais's job to clean up the mess, 'and that's making me laugh more'. Inevitably, it was Merchant who gave in and went to get a dustpan and brush. 'But the point I wanted to make about that story is that there was no one else in the room, it was just the two of us. It wasn't like he was doing that to entertain anyone else. That was enough for him; pleasurable for him . . .'

Stephen was to find the BBC's Trainee Assistant Producer Scheme (TAPS) a far more stable, if somewhat less rib-tickling, proposition. Surprisingly, Ricky was still in the job at Xfm when, in June 1998, his erstwhile right-hand man returned with camera crew in tow to recapture some of their wacky humour for a short film that he needed to make for the course.

One of the requirements of the BBC scheme was for would-be producers to make a short feature. It was usual for trainees to tackle such serious subjects as drug addiction or homelessness, but Merchant took a different tack. He decided that he would bring a character called 'Seedy Boss' to the screen, the persona his Xfm employer Ricky Gervais had often assumed to entertain mates down the pub. Crucially, he also decided that Ricky would play the role on screen, despite his lack of acting experience. The fact that they only had the use of a camera crew for a single day meant that time was very much of the essence, and the resulting twenty-minute film was shot in Ricky's old office at the University of London Union. Although some of the details would be later changed – the short was set in the offices of a wood-pulp bleach and dye company in Staffordshire – Ricky was the centre of attention from the off.

Amazingly, this was the first time Gervais had ever written anything, let alone acted before a camera. And again, his *raison d'être* as a performer was to give the proposition a reality he rarely saw. 'I didn't know what I

From zero to hero: Despite a slow start to his show-business career, Ricky Gervais eventually hit the big time, from stand-up comedian to children's author, comedy writer and actor to radio presenter.

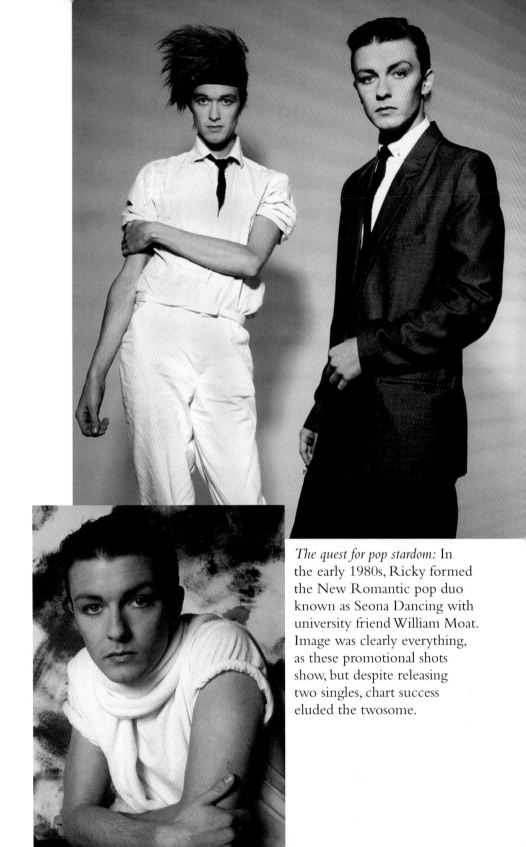

The quest for pop stardom: In the early 1980s, Ricky formed the New Romantic pop duo known as Seona Dancing with university friend William Moat. Image was clearly everything, as these promotional shots show, but despite releasing two singles, chart success eluded the twosome.

Above: After studying philosophy at the University of London, Ricky later returned there professionally when he became entertainments manager at the students' union, ULU. His years of employment there provided much source material for *The Office*.

In the early 1990s, Ricky briefly managed Suede, at the time an up-and-coming band that had yet to sign a record deal. (*From left to right:* Simon Gilbert, Bernard Butler, Brett Anderson and Mat Osman.)

Ricky's media career began with a fortuitous move to London-based independent radio station Xfm in the mid 1990s (*right*). The station was officially launched in September 1997, and although Ricky was made redundant almost a year later, he would be welcomed back with open arms in 2001.

Ricky first met his writing partner Stephen Merchant during his early radio days at Xfm. Although the fresh-faced young graduate did not stay at Ricky's side at Xfm for long, the two of them clearly hit it off, and remained friends until their paths crossed professionally once again.

Comedy heroes:
From childhood to
the present day,
Ricky has been an
ardent fan of the
slapstick humour of
Laurel and Hardy.

A keen follower of British
comedy series *Fawlty
Towers*, *Rising Damp* and
Porridge, Ricky also loved
to listen to the expletive-
filled commentaries of
cult wits Derek and Clive
(played by Dudley Moore
and Peter Cook).

In July 2001, *The Office* hit British screens for the first time. Written by Ricky Gervais and Stephen Merchant, it featured the former as David Brent, smug boss of Wernham Hogg, a paper-supply company in Slough.

Choosing the much-maligned Berkshire town for the location of the comedy series was clearly an inspired decision. The roundabout in central Slough (*below*) that features in the programme's opening credits has now become a famous landmark.

Stars of The Office: Since taking on the role of Gareth, Mackenzie Crook has appeared in numerous Hollywood films, most notably *Pirates of the Caribbean* alongside Johnny Depp and Keira Knightley (*above right*). After leaving behind her receptionist's duties, Lucy Davis (*below*) played a major role in the successful British zom-rom-com *Shaun of the Dead*, while Martin Freeman (*right*) has featured in a number of television comedies as well as several films, including *The Hitchhiker's Guide to the Galaxy*.

wanted exactly,' he later admitted, 'but I knew what I hated on telly.' No fan of over-acting, he refused to re-take scenes he felt caught the mood he sought.

He played a jovially overbearing managing director with pretensions to being an entertainer, rather than the deluded middle manager later to enter the hearts of the nation. The documentary style was down to the economics of the production – Merchant and co. only had a camera crew for a day, so it had to be shot quickly. The fly-on-the-wall approach let them get away with problems like extraneous noise and poor lighting, and with lots of straight-to-camera interviews there were no lengthy set-ups.

The plot was simple. Receptionist June (acted in the short by Nicola Cotter, who would later turn up as Ricky's secretary in the first series of *The Office*) played a harmless prank on her boss before being sacked by him and accusing him of being a 'pervert'. It also starred Merchant (who provided the introductory voice-over) as the office joker. The film's tone was somewhat harsher than that of the subsequent TV series, but much of the material was carried over into the first episode proper. Among the dialogue and scenes that survived included Brent organizing a job for a forklift-truck operator – and the classic line, 'Some people say I'm the best boss. They go to me, "We've never worked in a place like this. You're such a laugh. You get the best out of us." And I go, "C'est la vie. If that's true – excellent."'

Working in offices for people like the Seedy Boss was, Merchant explained to the *Bristol Evening Post*, something they had in common: 'We started talking about it when I first met Ricky at Xfm and how there are always the same type of characters in every office. There is always someone who thinks he is the funniest person in the world or someone who has dreams of bigger and better things. There is always an argument in an office about who the stapler belongs to and people Tippex their names on them. It is only when you start to think about it that you realize how amusing it is.'

If Xfm had been a wacky place to inhabit, Merchant found his new working environment gave him even more food for thought. 'Even in the BBC, people still Tippexed their names on the back of their chairs so no one would nick them. All newcomers are shown a three-hour health and safety video, but all I remember is it teaching you not to pour coffee down the back of your computer monitor.'

When Stephen and Ricky first put their heads together to film *Seedy Boss*, it was very much the time of the docu-soap. *Airport, Hotel, Driving School* – there had been a glut of documentaries serving up life stories in neat, half-hour segments with an avuncular voice-over to smooth out any of life's unfortunate infelicities. A number of participants, notably Jeremy Spake (the Russian-speaking and – coincidentally? – goatee-bearded star of *Airport*) and Maureen Rees (the Cardiff cleaner who became the unfortunate 'star pupil' of *Driving School*), started popping up elsewhere on television, not only leading to confusion but also feeding Gervais's imagination.

'That was one of our themes, that you could become famous overnight,' he explained. He mocked how, when 'normal people get their platform, they think, This is it, I'll get an agent, I'll probably go on Channel Five. And then they open their mouth and blow it.' (Several years later, the arrival of *Big Brother* and the likes of Jade Goody and Chantelle would prove Ricky right in an even bigger way.)

After the film demo had been completed, Merchant wasted no time in exploiting his contacts at the Beeb and circulated a tape, but initially there was very little enthusiasm. However, his luck was set to change when producer Ash Atalla saw its potential, and although it would be some time before momentum with the project gathered speed, the rollercoaster ride to fame was just about to begin.

4

Late-night Lunacy

❛ I don't do anything different on telly from what I do in pubs or at home . . . If you can still do it without clamming up in front of a camera, it becomes a job. ❜

AN OFT-REPEATED QUESTION in any interview with Ricky Gervais is: Where does Ricky end and David Brent begin? While the man himself sees a clear dividing line between himself and his creation, interviewers have often been left wondering. The division was even less clear in Ricky's TV talk-show days, when his persona as the eponymous host was often taken to reflect his own views.

His relationship with the small screen began in September 1998 with him playing a clearly defined part, yet the star of the programme in Channel 4's *Comedy Lab* strand – middle-aged, David Bowie-obsessed Clive Meadows – was close enough to himself to suggest he'd borne in mind the advice he'd been given by Mr Taylor at Ashmead School: 'Write what you know.' Chrono-logically speaking, Meadows was to be first in Gervais's gallery of awkward, socially inept losers that continued with Brent and Millman.

Even more fascinatingly, the one-off show entitled *Golden Years*, which was co-written with Stephen Merchant, focused on a thirty-something manager (of a video store rather than an office) who goes through a mid-life crisis and is obsessed with the idea of appearing on cheesy TV talent show *Stars In Their Eyes* . . . as who else but David Bowie?

In the words of noted comedy critic Mark Lewisohn, 'The reaction of his colleagues (he works in a video store) ranges from supportive (his secretary Zoe) to obstructive (his partner Barry), but Clive perseveres. Then he fails to get the TV slot and alienates Zoe by his gauche treatment of her as a sex object when showing off to a fellow 'artist' – Freddie Mercury lookalike Ian Croft.'

Nicholas Hutchison played the part of Barry and Zoe was played by Amelia Curtis. With jobs for the boys in mind, Killer Queen frontman Pat Myers starred as Ian 'Freddie' Croft, while even Stephen Merchant managed to score himself a bit-part as a character called James. The show aired at 10.55 p.m. on Wednesday 8 September and, to this writer's knowledge, has never been repeated, despite Gervais's subsequent fame. Lewisohn's conclusion: '*Golden Years* (a Bowie song title) had some good moments, but the central character's unadulterated lack of warmth worked against it.'

One Internet critic concurred: 'It was pretty weak, but you could see the germination of *The Office* in it.' He reckoned the highlight was Gervais 'trying to sing along to "Space Oddity" and do both double-tracked vocals together'.

The programme strand had also offered Johnny Vegas his first appearance on TV, so *Comedy Lab* could claim to have played a part in encouraging two successful careers, as well as resulting in an inevitably high number of failures.

Others to pass through the *Lab* included Dom Joly and Jimmy Carr, who would link with Ricky as a contributing writer on his forthcoming chat show. 'Channel 4 is rare in taking risks and giving people a chance,' said Carr, 'and *The Comedy Lab* is a godsend for stand-up comedians who would never otherwise have a half-hour slot on television.' Carr would follow Gervais's path by writing a series, *Your Face or Mine*, which he was uniquely qualified to present. 'The channel ran through a list of comedians but they were all too nice to insult members of the general public. Then they thought of me.'

Coincidentally, with the screening of *Golden Years* in September 1998 came the launch, on Channel 4, of *The 11 O'Clock Show*. In the tradition of *Not the Nine O'Clock News*, it was broadcast three times weekly as an 'alternative' news programme that made the most of its topicality by being written on the morning of transmission. This did, however, lead to a certain amount of 'lowest common denominator' material creeping in.

By the time the second series arrived on screen early in 1999, original presenters Fred MacAulay and Brendon Burns had been replaced by Iain Lee and Daisy Donovan. Spoof interviews with time-expired celebrities by Sacha Baron Cohen interspersed the sketches and enabled him to develop his successful Anglo-Asian Ali G character. It was inevitable that he would outgrow the format, just as *The Simpsons* outgrew *The Tracey Ullman Show*, and in 1999 *The 11 O'Clock Show*'s producers were faced with finding a replacement for their want-away star.

They had heard Ricky on the radio, and according to Stephen Merchant they had also seen the demo tape of *Seedy Boss* that had been made for his BBC course. Duly impressed with what they had seen and heard, they called him in to fill the unenviable role of replacement. 'I love Ali's work,' said an (at least publicly) undaunted Gervais, 'but I think I got the job because I was much fatter and older than any of the producers.' The producers in turn took their revenge by inventing a spoof biography for the new cast member on the show's website that suggested he'd been a pizza delivery man who'd once knocked down an old lady while speeding on his moped. Like most of the few 'personal' details to reach the public domain, this has since been endlessly recycled to Ricky's chagrin.

He believed it was the fact that he 'took the mickey out of DJ-speak and made a joke out of how bad I was at my job' that won him the chance to appear in vision as well as sound. 'I'd just DJ in my normal voice – I used to go in, put my feet up and when the mike came on, just say, "What?"'

He found he had the confidence to appear in front of the camera, not to mention an audience, and the opportunity he was given, to play the part of a roving reporter, allowed him to deal with any teething problems in a relatively obscure location. His task was to replace Ali G's segments with topical inserts, delivered from the standpoint of a bigoted journalist. One slight problem, he admitted later in a *Guardian* questionnaire on his 'media consumption habits', was that, 'I'm not a news pundit. I could talk all day about telly, but reading newspapers passes me by a bit. I'm too lazy to read them. The only time I read the papers was when I did *The 11 O'Clock Show*, and even then other people read the stories to me, or I just made them up.'

For the first time in his life, however, he found that he was not only reading the papers but also featuring in them, as TV reviewers demanded to know if he was actually for real or if the spoof news reporter was playing the role for laughs. The *Coventry Evening Telegraph* went in search of its own scoop in February 2000, and found a man who claimed to be 'well up on bar-room philosophy'.

'I'm the last person who should be talking about politics, or women's issues or whatever,' Ricky explained, referring to his TV character. 'Pretty soon it's revealed that I'm an opinionated bigot, a bit of an idiot really. So I slag off the group who I don't think should benefit from a National Lottery grant, and it's not long before I reveal things about myself that I don't really mean to.'

He took his mother's down-to-earth sense of humour as his inspiration – most notably the fact that Eva Gervais had a view on all subjects. Her opinion of *The 11 O'Clock Show*, however, was unrepeatable, and she was horrified by her son's appearance as the foul-mouthed reporter. 'She used to tell me my language was disgusting and asked why I didn't do something nice,' Ricky has revealed.

Nor was his mother alone in her reaction to the show, as viewers complained in their droves about Ricky's comic material. However, just as many others begged to differ and insisted he was the funniest thing in the show. 'Most of the people who were saying it was horrendous –

and it was, that was the joke – wouldn't have minded if I'd had a wig on and called myself Billy the Bigot from Bermondsey. I thought I'd made it obvious: did anyone really believe I thought the disabled were lazy or famine was funny?' he asked *The Observer*'s Geraldine Bedell.

Sample humour included branding suffragettes 'mental bean-flickers', claiming the crowd at the Derby cheered as a protesting suffragette got trampled to death by the King's horse because 'it was the first time the lezza had ever been jumped', and asking, 'How big an animal could you kick to death? A dog? How *big* a dog?'

Ricky would later lament in the *Evening Standard* that he wished he'd used a name other than his own: 'Warren Mitchell was obviously not Alf Garnett, and Sacha Baron Cohen isn't Ali G. But my character was called Ricky Gervais, and there was a horrible risk that I might have been taken up as the new Bernard Manning.

'David Baddiel once said that comedy is your conscience having a day off, but that's not true. You must censor yourself; it's all about who's in earshot. I am an atheist, but I don't run cackling into churches going: "There's no God!" Even if you're in the right, you don't upset people for the fun of it.'

But people were undoubtedly upset by his efforts at humour. Caitlin Moran of *The Times* was one, and she mounted an erudite condemnation of a show she believed confused humour with cynicism. Her conclusion was that the show was being championed by 'an unnamed Channel 4 executive who . . . has spent the past fifteen years of his career being teased by his hard mates for working for a channel that has Lesbian Weekends, and has finally snapped . . .' If not, she concluded, 'C4 should have pulled the programme months ago . . . I found *Duck Patrol* more amusing.'

The fact that Gervais's routine was based on being offensive rather than naïve and wacky, as Ali G had been, impacted on main presenters Donovan and Lee, who were obliged to tone down their own personas to provide an effective contrast. A relaunch with new presenters failed, and by the end of 2000 *The 11 O'Clock Show* was a footnote in televisual history. Fascinatingly, however, it would not be Donovan (still merely a peripheral TV figure, despite the advantage of being the daughter of late celebrity photographer and film-maker Terence Donovan) and Lee (who presents celebrity scandal documentaries and video game review shows) who flourished, but 'bit-part players' Baron Cohen and Gervais. Quite possibly, *The 11 O'Clock Show* was something it was better not to be indelibly associated with.

When Channel 4 had recommissioned the show, Ricky announced via *The Observer* that his character was going to be 'more obviously satirical, trying to improve television. He thinks he can put the world to rights. It'll be much more of a cartoon, a *Viz*-type character, not just borrowing bits of philosophy from the pub, but verging on the delusional and mentally ill.'

Viewers did not sit on the fence when it came to Ricky's contributions, and with the Internet fast becoming a soapbox for comedy connoisseurs and others, his deliberate obnoxiousness, coupled with remarks such as 'The Falklands is my favourite war.' understandably prompted strong reactions. One contributor to a comedy website discussion made his feelings known. 'I hate Ricky Gervais,' he wrote. 'He is sick, infantile and not at all funny. Chuck him off the show and replace him with more Iain Lee, please.' His mother's comment: 'Yes, son, very good, but why do you have to swear so much? I don't know where you get it from, you cheeky little bleeder.'

While there were professional critics like Caitlin Moran who believed that 'when Ali G left the show, so did the discerning viewer', Ricky had been well enough received for the channel to entrust him with his own series. It would be late-night, which would encourage gratuitous swearing. More importantly, it would give Gervais and Merchant their first vehicle by which to reach the British public on more than a one-off basis.

One thing the show would not touch was politics. As he explained to *The Observer*, 'years and years standing round a student bar hearing bad comedians getting rounds of applause' had cured Ricky of any interest in incorporating such material into his act. He also revealed that he had always wanted to perform at the Comedy Store, to test out these theories, but he could never quite summon up the bottle. 'I could not bear to stand up there and be unfunny. Couldn't have coped with it.'

Unfortunately for Ricky, he would find himself having to deal something far more distressing when, in January 2000, his mother Eva died. Aged seventy-four, she was the victim of lung cancer, and her passing understandably hit her youngest son hard. Yet he was full of admiration for how she dealt with death. 'She coped well. I think she thought she would get better. But we could see her going downhill.' Partner Jane told the *Mirror* that for Ricky, the youngest of the family, 'it was a very emotional time'. Ricky had been a smoker for a while, but had already given up a habit he later described as 'absolutely pointless . . . At least beer does something to you.'

A few months later the family would gather together once again, but this time for happier reasons. Ricky had informed his nearest and dearest that Reading University had invited him, as the town's local TV celebrity, to make an after-dinner speech. Given his *11 O'Clock Show* history, it could have been expected to be a little near the knuckle. He asked his family to come along as well, but he also warned them to be on their best behaviour. Brother Bob, now a painter and decorator living in Wokingham, took exception to the instruction 'Look smartish, and don't embarrass me.' It was a red rag to a bull.

Bob explained how the event panned out: 'I said, "Course not," and immediately went out and got a T-shirt printed with "You're a ****" written on the front. I put a jacket over the top and zipped it up, and off we went.

'Ricky kept saying, "Please, it's important, don't do anything to show me up, please behave yourself." We went through these doors, and it turned out to be my surprise fiftieth birthday party. I looked around at Ricky in shock, and he unzipped his own jacket to reveal a T-shirt that said, "No, Bob, *you're* the ****."'

Clearly, despite the passing of many years since childhood, the family tradition of making jokes at each other's expense was very much alive and flourishing in the new millennium.

Perhaps as a response to his mother's death, or simply because he had become more conscious of his health, by the start of the twenty-first century, exercise had found its way into Ricky's busy schedule. At the age of thirty he had been a trim ten stone, but had apparently put on three more in the intervening nine years. At five foot eight, he acknowledged he could 'lose a stone. But I'm overweight, I'm not obese.' In a *Wales on Sunday* health questionnaire, he confessed he was 'getting less happy' with his body, but conceded that there was 'nothing I can do about it, really'. He'd never been in hospital and would only consult a doctor 'when I think I'm going to die. If my arm was hanging off I might go.'

His new regime was to take a twenty-minute run three times a week ('Just enough to break into a sweat and make my heart remember what it's meant to do'), then return to spend ten minutes punching a boxing dummy called a slam man – one way to hit back at his critics. His typically jocular explanation of this new regime was that this daily practice earned him the right to 'eat a pizza, drink lots of pints and lay on the couch'. In a few years' time he would find himself the target of paparazzi lenses and, worse yet, students with water bombs, but for now he could jog the Bloomsbury streets unmolested.

Fame was, however, very much on the horizon as Ricky Gervais, bar-room philosopher and spoof news reporter, became a chat-show host.

Launched in September 2000 on Channel 4, *Meet Ricky Gervais* was a deliberate attempt to appear amateurish and lovable. Scripted with Stephen Merchant, with additional material from Jimmy Carr and Robin Ince, it made a virtue out of having a bargain-basement imitation of a Parkinson/Wogan-style chat-show set. The requisite three armchairs, for instance, had, he claimed, been recycled from such shows as *The Two Ronnies* (Ronnie Corbett's close-to-the-ground effort) and *Only Fools and Horses* ('It's Grandad's . . . and it's still wet'). The functional, if seemingly unfinished, backdrop had supposedly come into being when Channel 4 told him he could keep what he didn't spend of his budget, while the *Meet Ricky Gervais* logo was scrawled in a childish hand.

Meet Ricky Gervais had no theme tune. The show would open with the 'sweeping second hand' screen as he improvised over the top or bickered with his director as to what should be playing as he made his entrance. A uniform of T-shirt and casual trousers made him look slightly ill at ease, an image added to by his pasty complexion. In many ways, the closest parallel was with Caroline Aherne's *The Mrs Merton Show*, where the host herself was the star, the interviewees merely the adornments and accessories. *Meet Ricky Gervais* was an invitation to the public to make *his* acquaintance, rather than that of his 'guests': they would certainly learn more about him and his supposed views than the activities of those he was questioning.

The concept was to exaggerate the nastier attributes of the chat-show host, just as his *11 O'Clock Show* persona had been the predatory man with the roving microphone. But this was something his 'victims' had to be aware of. 'I had a word with all the guests before we started filming the show and said, "Look, it's just a character, so don't chin me,"' Ricky explained.

The public at large seemed not to get the joke, which left Ricky nonplussed, as he explained to *The Sun*'s Giovanna Iozzi: 'I was surprised when some people really thought I believed the handicapped were lazy or that world starvation was funny after I said it in my act. It's because I used my own name and don't dress up like Ali G or Mrs Merton. I'm sure that was a mistake . . . It

79

worries me if I've offended individuals. But the most frightening thing is when people agree with what my character says and don't realize it's a joke.'

This was in truth no chat show, but a series of scripted stories which Ricky would shoehorn into the interview, whether the subject was complicit or not. This was apparent at the very start of the first show, featuring two very different personalities in garden guru Tommy Walsh of *Ground Force* fame and veteran DJ/tireless charity worker Jimmy Savile. One TV website, which claimed that the show flopped because Ricky 'couldn't get any decent guests', reckoned Walsh and Savile were as good as it got!

Walsh, still on the first lap of small-screen stardom, immediately sussed how the game was played and obediently sat by as Ricky went off on his own flights of fancy. Sir James was another matter entirely.

Having started on the wrong foot by likening him to an ageing Leeds prostitute – the debut of a running gag from that first show onwards in which Ricky's celebrity booker made him guess who the week's guests were by describing their apparel and personalities – Gervais found himself totally outmanoeuvred by the show-business veteran. The running themes of the interview were to be age and charity, with Ricky poking fun at both. Jimmy admitted he was nearer to one hundred years of age than his host – 'even though it doesn't look like it' – and fended off jokes about his reserved room at Broadmoor mental hospital with good grace.

After some tasteless remarks about betting on the Special Olympics ('because every competitor's a winner'), occasioned purely by the fact that Savile's father had been a bookie's runner, the camera panned to show the two guests' reactions. Tommy Walsh was obligingly doubled over with mirth, while Jimmy chomped on his cigar. On the cessation of the audience laughter, Savile remarked sagely (and to more mirth), 'This is the man with the shortest series in the world.'

The fact was that *Meet Ricky Gervais* simply tried too hard. The guest list was paper thin. 'The problem is either they hadn't heard of me – or they had,' said Gervais. Other features included a mini-interview with a member of the audience that inevitably went wrong, and a closing game-show parody.

Most curious of all set-pieces, perhaps, was the recruitment of Tony Green, co-host and darts commentator from the televised darts show *Bullseye*, whose job was to stand by a (never-used) dartboard and interject occasionally when invited to by his host. He would occasionally roll out his trademark 'One hundred and eight-yyyyyyyy' catchphrase.

The show's obligatory ad break would be followed by a supposed snatch of dressing-room footage featuring Ricky and a sinister-looking Stephen Merchant playing a Channel 4 'suit' with predatory sexual tendencies. Following this strange and deliberately unsettling interlude, a seemingly unaffected Ricky would re-emerge from behind the lattice backdrop to introduce his second guest.

Gervais's other guests in the show's six-week run were singer Midge Ure, chef Antony Worrall Thompson, snooker player John Virgo, film director Michael Winner, designer Wayne Hemingway, US actress Stefanie Powers and TV magician Paul Daniels. Interestingly, TV presenters would comprise the most numerous of his 'victims', including Peter Purves, Penny Smith and Tony Hart.

And he already had a wish list for a potential second series. 'I'd love to get [Labour deputy leader] John Prescott on, though I'd have to be careful – he's got a good left hook. But if he looked keen to hit me, I'd throw him a pie to distract him.'

Actress Stefanie Powers initially turned him down. 'She was probably doing something – anything – else,' he said, before she relented. She doubtless wished she *had* stayed away when Ricky compared her to mass murderer's wife Rosemary West on the grounds that her most famous show, *Hart to Hart*, carried the tag line, 'When they met, it was murder.'

Predictably, the press fell upon *Meet Ricky Gervais* like a shoal of malnourished piranhas. While opprobrium from the *Daily Mail* (whose right-wing political leanings Ricky affected not to be aware of) would have been expected, Charlie Catchpole of the *Daily Mirror* was a bigger fish by far. The headline for his column four days after the first show, 'Sad To Meet You, Ricky', said it all. The next day saw *The Sun*'s Garry Bushell develop into the most unlikely occupant of moral high ground. 'Outrage by numbers' was the far-right punk rocker turned TV critic's expert assessment of *Meet Ricky Gervais*. And there was more . . .

But Ricky remained, publicly at least, bullish in the face of such beastly critical broadsides. 'Jimmy Savile said that the show would have the shortest run in history! But he was wrong,' he cackled. 'We're doing a second series!' As it happened, though, events overtook Ricky and this never occurred. His final assessment of the series as it ended: 'If you don't get complaints at 11 p.m. on Channel 4 you are doing something wrong.'

Looking back in 2001, he admitted to *The Sunday Times* that it had been 'probably stupid and potentially damaging to use my own name, but I think it was brave as well. I hope it was obvious I was playing a character and being an idiot with ridiculous ideas . . . You have to have a bit of an edge, otherwise I might as well have "satire" written all over my shirt.' While he claims he was misunderstood, the confusion he encountered in this early period of his performing life would remain a hurdle to cross. As would the infantile obsession with 'mongs', 'gays' and 'lezzas' that had so infuriated Caitlin Moran.

(Interestingly, once secure in his post-*Office* fame, he was not afraid to reveal more of his true feelings to gay magazine *Attitude*. 'I wouldn't use a derogatory term or euphemism unless it was ironic,' he said, explaining that, 'I would never say "homosexual" – it sounds like something clinical from the sixties.' But his worst moment came when he had to do a glossary of British words for the US *Office* DVD. 'I had to explain the word "bender". I was at this serious meeting and I was like, "Bender is a derogatory term for a gay man. It's derived . . . probably because gay men bend over." And then a gay guy there said, "No, actually it's from the eighties' 'gender bender'." I wanted to crawl in a hole and die.')

Having left radio behind with Xfm in October 1998, Ricky had found himself with a redundancy cheque and time on his hands to put together his *Seedy Boss* project. He kept his hand in by making a few guest appearances on Mary Anne Hobbs's Radio 1 show, but this was to be a brief run. Even briefer was a one-off Radio 1 show with Sara Cox promoting 1999's Glastonbury Festival.

He made guest appearances in such shows as *Vic Reeves Examines, Comedy Cafe* and as a call-centre worker in Channel 4's *Spaced*. He also graced the table at the same channel's *Celebrity Late Night Poker,* but disgraced himself by managing to exit the competition before all his fellow celebs, including Martin Amis, Victoria Coren and Stephen Fry.

While work was up and down, his relationship with Jane was the bedrock on which he could rely. 'We've always got on really, really well,' she told *The Sun* in 2002, 'and I have always hoped it would be for ever. He has always made me laugh and when you come back after a long day at work it is great to have someone at home you can laugh with.'

Living with an up-and-coming TV producer also meant he didn't have to go far for advice. 'I didn't go in making ridiculous mistakes. I suppose if you live with a doctor you'd probably know a bit. You'd be able to say, "I know what *that* is – it's shingles!"'

The couple have never married and, through choice, have no children. 'If Ricky got down on one knee to propose, I'd probably laugh,' said Jane, while Gervais has claimed they've always been 'too busy to have kids. We're not going to wake up at sixty-five and think, God, we didn't have kids. Maybe I've never grown up myself. Besides, I'd be terrified. I'd wake up every night in a cold sweat worrying [whether] they were still breathing.'

Jane, whose curriculum vitae includes stints as producer of *This Life* and *Teachers,* is 'really proud of what he has achieved. He is such a clever guy. Ricky has more ideas than anyone I've ever met. Every day he'll say, "Oh my God, I've got a fantastic idea," and they are nearly always really good, which is very irritating.'

One of Jane's good ideas was to enrol Ricky as music adviser on *This Life*, a show that depicted a rather more upper-crust stratum of young London society than the student circles she and Ricky had inhabited. Premiered in March 1996, it concerned a group of attractive, if badly behaved, lawyers living in an upmarket London house lurching from one emotional crisis to another: one critic described it as 'a British *thirtysomething*, *Friends* and *Ally McBeal* all rolled into one'. With its jerky close-ups and trendy music (selected by you know who), it was a surprise ratings success. Thirty-two episodes saw it through to the summer of 1997 on BBC2. Little had Jane or Ricky known then that he would be breaking ratings records on that self-same channel a few years later.

Two and a half years after losing his mother, Ricky said farewell to dad Jerry. As Jane explained, it was less of a shock than his mother's death. 'Jerry was over eighty now, and had had a couple of strokes. Ricky went to visit as much as he could, it was a very tough time for him, it is awful, but his family helped a lot – they cheered each other up.'

It wasn't the Gervais family way to be down for long, however, and the atmosphere at the funeral was one of celebration of a life. 'Jerry wouldn't have allowed misery,' said family friend and former school mate Ricky Bell. 'I have never been to a funeral where there was so much laughter. Ricky had everyone in stitches. It was just the way Jerry wanted it. Ricky was holding court in the front room afterwards, talking about his mum and dad, and the holidays from hell in the caravan.'

Ricky was philosophical about his father dying. 'He slowed down once my mum died and for the last six months things gave up,' he revealed to *The Sun.* 'He was eighty-two and had been ill for quite a while. You're upset but you don't feel the same. If he had been fifty-five it would have been a different kettle of fish – that's a tragedy. But to drink rum and smoke roll-ups until you're eighty-two . . . Well done to him.'

As an atheist, he felt the worst thing wasn't dying, but 'how you go': 'If there was a God, I'd like them to say, "Rick, I'm not going to tell you when you're going to die. But you're just going to go to sleep one night and not wake up."'

While he's alive and kicking, Ricky has lent his fame to some worthwhile causes. In 2001, he provided the voice for a £190,000 government drink-driving campaign, a televised boxing match the following year was to raise money for Macmillan cancer nurses and he's delivered a radio ad for prostate cancer, attempting to use humour to raise awareness of the killer disease. He would never claim to be a Bob Geldof, but Ricky has done his bit . . . while reserving the right to poke fun at himself and other do-gooders.

Yet the celebrity status he lent to these causes would not have accrued without his first TV series. It's true to say that the half-hour of television broadcast on 9 July 2001 would change not only Ricky Gervais's life, but the history of UK television comedy. *The Office* was about to open for business . . .

5

Open for Business

I know I'm probably not the best actor, writer or director. But I like being able to do all three. It's like building a model toy. What's the point in buying it and getting somebody else to put it together? Where's the fun in that?

ON THE FACE OF IT, setting a sitcom in an office environment was nothing new. There had been series about clerical workers since the early 1960s with the likes of *Here's Harry*, starring bespectacled bumbler Harry Worth, and David Nobbs's highly successful and often surreal parody of white-collar life, *The Fall and Rise of Reginald Perrin*, starring the late, great Leonard Rossiter.

The last twenty-five years had seen such programmes as *Kiss Me Kate*, *The Creatives* and *High Stakes* adding their names to the genre. And only months before *The Office*'s first appearance came the six-episode run of *Office Gossip*, set in the head office of a toy company and starring *Birds of a Feather*'s Pauline Quirke as put-upon PA Jo Thomas.

And who could forget Charlie Higson's monstrous office practical joker Colin Hunt in *The Fast Show*?

So the premise of yet another workplace-based comedy drama would surely not have been much of an appetizing proposition to TV bosses. Equally, there had already been a number of spoof documentary-style series such as *People Like Us* and *Operation Good Guys*. Given this background, the genesis of what was to become one of the biggest TV successes of the new millennium was not exactly promising.

Stephen Merchant's decision to enrol on the trainee assistant producer course was the catalyst for what was to come. He began to mix in the right circles, rubbing shoulders with influential figures who would play an important role in bringing *The Office* to an audience: individuals such as BBC Head of Entertainment Paul Jackson and Head of Comedy Entertainment Jon Plowman. Merchant also got involved with sketch show *Comedy Nation*, where he encountered future *Office* producer Ash Atalla.

Although his demo tape wasn't immediately fallen upon by talent-hungry TV executives, one individual who did express an interest was the aforementioned Atalla, who was by then working as a junior TV comedy producer on the disability-based show *Yes Sir, I Can Boogie*. He thought Gervais 'brilliant . . . The twitches of his face, the small movements of his eyes.' Atalla thought he might be on to something, even though Plowman's early reaction to the short was cool. So he approached established comedy producer Anil Gupta, at the time riding the crest of a wave with the success of 'Asian *Fast Show*' sketch programme *Goodness Gracious Me*.

Gupta saw the potential too, and agreed to try to push it around the corridors at White City. His first stop was the office of Jon Plowman. When Gupta was insistent that the corporation at least make a pilot episode, Plowman was a little less resistant than previously, but maintained that Ricky shouldn't play the lead role. It was considered that he wasn't well known enough to anchor a new series, especially one as downbeat as this, but Anil Gupta's enthusiasm ground him down. Plowman also felt that David Brent was too unlikeable a character, and people would never understand how he could get to such a position of power in the first place.

Gervais and Merchant had acquired a useful ally: Gupta bridged the gap between the young production end of the Beeb and the powers-that-be like Plowman, who remained unsure where it would lead even if he agreed to a pilot. Meanwhile, as the tape continued to do the rounds, Gervais had landed a role in Channel 4's fourth series of *The 11 O'Clock Show*.

Plowman eventually decided the twenty-minute teaser had some potential after all and as he later recalled, 'I gave them some money to go away and develop a script.' The development took several months of hard work and the writing duo was often reluctant to accept any con-structive suggestions from anyone at the BBC, even their champions. 'Ricky and Steve are extremely talented,' Gupta explained to Ben Walters in his BFI book, *The Office*, 'and very bright blokes, but their first reaction to being told something is to say "f**k off".'

Gupta and Atalla were insistent that the pilot had to have a strong storyline as well as the characterizations. And it was they who also pushed for the romance element, which later emerged as the classic love triangle between characters Tim, Dawn and her boyfriend Lee – Ricky would joke that they drew heavily on the situation between Humphrey Bogart, Ingrid Bergman and Paul Henreid in *Casablanca* for this! Credit, however, must be shared.

A lot of inspiration for the show, and the love story especially, came from big Hollywood movies such as the closing scenes of *The Bridges of Madison County* – 'When you think she's going to maybe go and pursue this other life and then realize she isn't,' as Gervais explained to *The Independent Magazine*. Or the sequence in Billy Wilder's *The Apartment*, where Shirley MacLaine says she noticed Jack Lemmon because he was 'the only man who ever took his hat off in the elevator'. 'There's no exposition,' quipped Ricky. 'Don't expose things completely.'

In addition to *Casablanca*, Gervais cited as favourites and influences *The Godfather* ('Amazing epic tale, the dynamics of the family and the world they live in is so wonderfully depicted. I love the fact that there's an ambiguity as to whether you should like these characters even though they're murderers'); *One Flew Over the Cuckoo's Nest* ('Jack Nicholson is the coolest. I saw him once at the Globes, walking around like a granddad at a barbecue in his back garden. He's the alpha male, he's the man'); and *It's a Wonderful Life* ('It's a classic Christmas film. It really does provide vitamins for the human spirit. I'm a terrible atheist, but a sucker for an angel, and this makes you forget there is nastiness in the world').

Gervais and Merchant were also keen to stick with the mockumentary style of the TAPS short. 'There's nothing funnier than real-life documentaries,' Ricky would later say. 'They resonate more.' And rather than go for the angle that the jokes would come from a group of film-makers making a film about office life, they played it safe and concentrated on the characters and the situations they got themselves into. Despite their faith in Gervais and Merchant, Gupta and Atalla were still very pleasantly surprised by what they came up with. 'They came back with this script and it was like, "They've done it,"' Gupta told Ben Walters.

As well as developing the character of David Brent, they also introduced the potential romance between Tim and Dawn, and, to get the plotline going, the added threat of redundancy with the company considering closing the branch. 'They'd done all those things that they said they weren't going to do,' said Gupta, 'but actually they'd done them rather brilliantly. It was all in the first script really, almost from the first draft.'

With the script accepted, the next step was to get the BBC to approve a pilot. Jon Plowman first pitched *The Office* to BBC2 controller Jane Root in the summer of 2000, at a meeting where independent companies and in-house departments approach channel heads with 'offers' – a series of projects, some of which get accepted and some that don't.

On paper, *The Office*, set in a nondescript workplace somewhere in Slough with very little happening, didn't exactly look like a going concern. But Gupta and Atalla brought it to life by the simple but brilliant expedient of putting together a five-minute highlight tape from the original short film to accompany the presentation. This not only succeeded in grabbing Root's attention but, as she later recalled, gave her 'a sense that there was this great character here'.

So what was to become known to millions as *The Office* finally got the green light. A modest budget of £90,000 was allocated and the pilot programme went into production. What was particularly unusual was that, from the start, Gervais and Merchant dug their heels in over directing it themselves – this was considered highly unorthodox, not only by the Head of Comedy Entertainment, but even by series director Anil Gupta, given the pair's glaring lack of experience in this department.

It was far more usual to bring in a director who had done that kind of sitcom before. Merchant was not prepared to compromise, however, and with the zeal of a 'new boy' felt, 'We've *got* to direct this. It wasn't that we thought we were the best directors in the world, but we knew what we wanted to see on the telly.' In the end, Gupta acted as the director on paper while the actual production was much more of a collaborative effort between the trio.

A lot of time was spent in readying the best possible script for the pilot and casting for it. Yet as Merchant admitted to *The Independent Magazine*, 'We didn't know anything about casting. We just knew we had to get the best naturalistic actors ever.' The pair initially agreed with each other that they 'should get people who aren't actors – we'll get real people in to do it!' But as Merchant pointed out, 'The thing is, real people can't do it. In fact, most actors can't do it. The most flattering thing for us is when people think it's improvised.'

Merchant and Gervais were particularly adept at getting the best out of their actors in this respect. 'We keep on top of them,' joked Ricky, 'almost to the point of embarrassment. It's not necessarily that they're doing it wrong, just that sometimes there might be ten ways to do something and we want number seven.' As Merchant elaborated, 'Because we've acted it all out together in the writing room first, it's kind of like we know how every word should sound.'

Gervais admitted, however, that there was still the danger of the actors resenting taking direction from a couple of blokes who were learning as they went. 'When you're asking someone who's twice as good an actor as you, "Can you go up at the end of that sentence, because it's funnier?", that's where it gets trickier,' Merchant concurred. 'I don't know what the cast's opinion is of us as directors. I would imagine it's like we're pretending.'

Gervais and Merchant were equally fastidious in how they selected the actors to play the characters they'd created. While Ricky was already Brent incarnate, they looked long and hard to cast the roles of Dawn, Tim and Gareth. Gervais would later admit, 'We spent an awful lot of time on the script and casting because that's all we had.'

The part of Dawn was given quite early on to Lucy Davis, who, born in January 1973, was the daughter of one of the most enduring British comedians of the past thirty years, Jasper Carrott – although, as she would later insist to BBC America, she never played on this relationship to find employment. 'It doesn't really work. When I first started out it was just important that we kept our careers separate, largely because my dad had always been really private with his family.' Nonetheless, it didn't stop her from getting one of her earliest TV breaks in her father's hugely popular BBC series, *The Detectives*.

She had followed this up with work on such perennial series as *Holby City, Murder in Mind* and *Doctors*, as well as in costume dramas such as *Nicholas Nickleby* and *Pride and*

Prejudice, in which she played Maria Lucas. But perhaps her most famous role before she landed the job of Dawn Tinsley, the put-upon receptionist in *The Office*, was as Hayley Tucker in long-running radio soap *The Archers*, a part she only gave up when screen roles made it impossible to continue.

The subsequent success of *The Office* would assist her in landing a variety of more significant parts, such as Dianne, Simon Pegg's girlfriend in the hugely popular British zombie movie *Shaun of the Dead*, the voice of Sundance the Pig in *The Legend of the Tamworth Two*, and a role in the Johnny Vegas vehicle *Sex Lives of the Potato Men*.

The diversity of her acting career has, she says, been 'good for me as an actor because you like to play different roles, so you end up having quite a good show reel anyway'. Commenting on how she ended up playing Dawn, she recalled, 'It was December 1999 and I'd been up for a couple of pilots for the BBC, and this was one of them. It was the one I liked and I just thought I really wanted to be part of this, and fortunately that was the one that came through.'

For the role of Tim Canterbury, Gervais and Merchant eventually chose Martin Freeman, who had appeared in *Bruiser*, a BBC six-part comedy sketch series for which Ricky had written some material in 2000. Although he originally read for the part of Gareth Keenan, he was deemed much more suitable as Tim, the under-motivated sales rep, a beacon of sense and integrity in a sea of mediocrity, and a bloke who relieved the endless hours of boredom at Wernham Hogg by playing practical jokes on colleague Gareth (who repeatedly asked for Brent to take disciplinary measures against him). And he was not only frustrated by his job, but also by his unspoken feelings for Dawn.

Born in Aldershot in 1971, Freeman had made only a modest number of television appearances by the time he was recruited to *The Office*. However, his role in what was destined to become a hit British comedy would secure him subsequent parts in a number of mainstream films, including *Ali G Indahouse* (featuring Ricky's *11 O'Clock Show* predecessor), successful British movie *Love Actually*, and the sci-fi adventure film *The Hitchhiker's Guide to the Galaxy* (playing the reluctant hero Arthur Dent). Television offers also came flooding in, including the role of Lord Shaftesbury in period drama *Charles II: The Power and the Passion*, as well as significant parts in sitcoms *Hardware* and *The Robinsons*. Gervais and Merchant would later agree that, 'He is the person most sensible people are supposed to relate to . . . and, along with Dawn, the moral conscience of the show.'

Talking about his part to BBC America, Freeman explained: 'Tim is thoughtful and thwarted and intelligent and witty and a bit cowardly. I suppose the conceit of the thing was that he wanted to be the character the audience would most identify with as themselves. The nice thing about *The Office* is that all the characters in it are quite well rounded.

'As an actor you are asked to fit square pegs into round holes all the time in terms of the short cuts you have to take. Luckily, in *The Office* you end up taking virtually none. The scenes take their natural time. You do what people do in real life as opposed to doing what actors do with a mind to where that light is and where the camera is and hitting your mark.'

Elaborating further on his character, Freeman observed, 'I think Tim is very intelligent, but he doesn't have the bottle to actually get out and do what he wants to do, like properly ask Dawn out . . . or move, or leave the job. What I like about the character as well is that Tim is the one that everyone relates to, and he actually ends up doing what people do in real life, which is chicken out. He's not a hero, you know.'

Asked whether he would have liked to play another character in the show, he responded immediately, 'Yeah! David Brent. Ricky is not stupid; he's given himself the best f**king lines. But we all had really good stuff to say, genuinely we all had good ensemble stuff, but Ricky's no idiot and he's given himself some fantastic things to do that plays to all his strengths and makes people call him a comedy genius. The bastard!'

Completing the love triangle was warehouse worker Lee, played by actor Joel Beckett, who'd starred in TV series such as *Band of Brothers* and *Silent Witness,* and who would subsequently reap his own rewards from the success of *The Office* by getting parts in British films like *Green Street* and the role of Jake Moon in *EastEnders.* Speaking of the relationship between Dawn and Lee, the scriptwriters commented that they'd started going out with each other at fifteen and just settled into a comfortable routine. Marriage and kids seemed inevitable.

Perhaps the part of Gareth Keenan, former lieutenant in the Territorial Army and assistant to the regional manager, was the toughest to cast. Ricky and Stephen had originally envisaged him as a belligerent squaddie type – a far cry from the skeletal frame and sallow, slightly gormless looks of Mackenzie Crook, who would eventually land the part. A man once described as looking like 'a meerkat that's done ten rounds with John Prescott', Crook was born Paul Crook in September 1971 in Maidstone, Kent, but changed his name to Mackenzie when he discovered there was already a Paul Crook in the Equity book.

Having spent some eight years on the stand-up comedy circuit, his first break came when Bob Mortimer described him as 'the best character comedian around'. He subsequently became a comedy sketch contributor to *The 11 O'Clock Show* at a time when Ricky was also involved with the programme. In real life a shy, self-effacing and polite man, Crook admitted that like his *Office* character he was 'a bit of a pedant', and that he nearly always played those sorts of characters, such as on the show *TV To Go*, where he assumed the role of a very pedantic young man – good practice indeed for his role as the argumentative Gareth.

Talking of the role of the humourless Gareth on a BBC website, Gervais observed: 'Gareth Keenan really epitomizes men as boys. Men don't really grow up. And he's that person who's really stuck in a fourteen-year-old's body who thinks he could possibly survive a nuclear winter.' Crook based the role partly on the assistant manager of the Dartford branch of Pizza Hut where he worked after he'd done his A levels.

'It was quite a popular branch,' he told *The Daily Telegraph*. 'It won a few regional competitions. We had to say things to customers in a particular order – you couldn't move away from the script and this guy was obsessed by the rulebook. I painted Meatloaf's *Bat Out of Hell* album cover on the back of his leather jacket for him. A motorbike bursting out of a grave. It took me weeks. He paid me £25 for it . . . I remember the manager in Pizza Hut really did everything by the book. I suppose I should feel sorry for him. He really thought this is as good as it gets.'

Merchant and Gervais had seen Gareth physically different from the way he turned out, but both were impressed by his approach, especially the West Country accent that was put on for the part. In conversation with Ben Walters, Gervais commented, 'What was exciting about Mackenzie is because he looks very fragile and vulnerable, not like we first imagined. We found that we could give him more and more ridiculous and horrendous lines and you still don't mind because of his little bird-type face – like a little fledgling pigeon who hatched too early.'

Talking about Gareth, once described as the kid who would cross his fingers and pray to be left in charge of the class when the teacher was called away on an emergency, Crook later said to *The Observer*, 'Gareth was such a knob, but the part was so well written by Stephen and Ricky it was already all there on the page. You know, I almost didn't get the job. There were actually two of us up for Gareth, which I didn't realize till later. Me and a guy called Tim Presser, who's now a very good friend of mine. And it was really touch and go. I often think about this. Life would have been a bit different for the last few years.'

His joining the cast was a lucky break that would eventually pay dividends for his career – once the programme had become a success Crook was in big demand and would soon add a wealth of projects to his already impressive CV. As well as joining Lucy Davis in *Sex*

Lives of the Potato Men, he landed a number of roles in such films as *The Life and Death of Peter Sellers,* Terry Gilliam's *Brothers Grimm, Finding Neverland* and Michael Radford's 2004 adaptation of Shakespeare's *The Merchant of Venice.*

In 2003, in possibly his biggest film appearance to date, Crook was cast as Ragetti, a pirate with a wooden eye, in the Johnny Depp movies *Pirates of the Caribbean: The Curse of the Black Pearl* and its sequel *Dead Man's Chest.* He also outshone fellow actor Christian Slater when he played the challenging part of Billy Bibbit in the London West End production of Ken Kesey's *One Flew Over the Cuckoo's Nest.*

The cast of *The Office* was rounded out by a number of well-observed support roles, notably Ricky Howard, the temp played by Oliver Chris in the first series; Stirling Gallacher, who had originally appeared on *Meet Ricky Gervais,* who took on the role of the well-heeled Jennifer Taylor-Clarke, Brent's boss from Head Office; and Ralph Ineson, who played Chris Finch.

'Finchy', as Brent christened him, was the loud-mouthed, racist but highly rated travelling sales rep with an IQ of 142 who was also Brent's best mate and co-winner of six of Wernham Hogg's annual quiz nights. He was something of a success with the ladies, despite the never-ending stream of sexual innuendo he let loose. Ineson was already an experienced actor, having appeared in such big-budget films as *First Knight* and *From Hell* as well as TV series such as *Spooks* and *The Bill,* but like the other actors he would benefit immensely from appearing in *The Office,* landing the role of Zack in *Coronation Street.*

The part of the quiet, sullen, fat man, 'Big' Keith Bishop in the accounts department, was taken by Ewen MacIntosh, while Patrick Baladi played the well-liked Neil Godwin, the regional manager of the Swindon branch of Wernham Hogg, who was promoted to UK manager in the second series.

It was BBC production manager Judith Bantock who found the perfect location for the shoot – some dilapidated old office space near to Teddington Studios. There was little effort to improve the décor – Gervais insisted that the stains on the carpet contributed to the look and feel of the programme. Merchant and Gervais also stuck to their guns regarding the pace, and the only major thing that was added in post-production was a voice-over by former *Bergerac* star John Nettles, who was narrator on the highly popular BBC docu-soap *Airport*.

Reaction to the completed pilot was positive, if not over the top. There were a number of projects clamouring to go into full production at the BBC, and *The Office* was also up against the recommissioning of the spoof observational documentary series, *People Like Us*. It was all down to the decision made by the controller of BBC2, Jane Root, as to which would succeed.

The stars were obviously in the right configuration for Gervais and Merchant – Root opted to go with *The Office*, sensing that, after two series, *People Like Us* had run its course. But it was a close-run thing, as Jon Plowman had been more heavily involved in the latter series. However, the comparative cheapness of making *The Office* was a major factor in its finding favour with those in the corridors of power at Shepherd's Bush, and the project was also both fresh and challenging to market.

For the theme music, the programme's creators opted for Mike d'Abo's 'Handbags and Gladrags', written in the late 1960s. Previously successfully covered by Chris Farlowe and Rod Stewart in the 1970s, it was later returned to the charts by Welsh band Stereophonics – and though many assume this was *The Office*'s version, it was in fact a never-commercially-released recording by Big George Webley (of *Have I Got News For You* theme fame).

The six-episode first series of *The Office* was scheduled to screen on 9 July 2001. In the meantime, Gervais and Merchant had spent long hours getting the ebb and flow of the narrative just right. Once finished, the series was warmly received by the BBC executives, yet the first episode almost snuck out unnoticed.

Most television stations don't launch new products at the height of the holiday season, but where the first episode of *The Office* was concerned the BBC flew in the face of convention. There was no big press fanfare and reaction from the general public was more than muted – the first episode got an audience figure of just 1.2 million, and, as Ricky was later to remark in crowing fashion, the only programme to score worse on BBC2's schedule that summer was women's bowls.

The figures didn't improve much over the next two episodes either, but perhaps because of its low-key launch and the fact that journalists discovered it for themselves, *The Office* received good critical notices from the press almost immediately – especially from *The Guardian*, which praised it for being 'extremely promising'. With some careful trailering from the Beeb, figures actually did improve, the fifth episode breaching the magic two million mark. By the end of its first run, *The Observer* declared it 'scarily realistic, but hilarious', while *The Times* hailed it as 'Original and accurate and painfully funny – it will have every office in the country twitching with spasms of recognition. This is a gem.'

The first programme was never designed to hook a huge audience, and that was a potential stumbling block of massive proportions, since it was normally the case with new comedy shows that the first programme would grab the biggest slice of the cake and figures would tail off thereafter. The casual viewer might have been forgiven for thinking this was another real-life fly-on-the-wall documentary as, gazing straight at the camera, smug boss David Brent welcomed a BBC TV crew into the office of the Slough paper suppliers. At first, Brent seemed like just another typical middle manager, the type that could be found in workplaces all over the country, a man who thought he managed his staff well and got on with them. But slowly the camera began to dig underneath this veneer to reveal a more sordid reality.

In the first scene he swung Alex, a new recruit, a job in the warehouse via some banal banter with Sammy, the warehouse supervisor. Having presented the other main members of the team – Dawn, Tim and Gareth – to the TV crew, after bragging about his drunken exploits from the night before, he slyly introduced his boss Jennifer Taylor-Clarke via his trademark talking head to camera with the quip 'aka Camilla Parker Bowles'.

A conversation between the two then introduced one of the main themes that would run through the rest of the series, the threat of redundancy: there were plans to close either the Slough or the Swindon offices. Lying through his teeth, Brent allayed any fears of job losses at a staff meeting and the air of despondency was momentarily dispelled by the first of a series of running gags in the relationship between Tim and Gareth, when Tim set the latter's stapler in a jelly mould.

After a series of scenes highlighting Brent's appalling people skills, the programme ended on a moment of intense awkwardness, when the ever-jovial but horrendously tactless manager pretended to sack Dawn in an attempt to show Ricky the temp the sort of practical jokes that were played in the office. It was an ill-conceived stunt that naturally backfired – with echoes of the equally embarrassing sequence in *The Fast Show* where Colin Hunt's workmates turned the tables on the office's arch prankster and got him the sack – and was an incident that revealed the bungling, dark side of a man who mistakenly thought of himself as a good human being and boss.

Over the next few episodes the documentary style would effortlessly reveal the politics of office life at Wernham Hogg, teasing out the relationships between the various workers and exposing the soft white underbelly of David Brent as the deluded yet complex buffoon and pretender he really was. While Brent tried to maintain an air of political correctness, the male behaviour around him was generally sexist and rife with innuendo, and he would often find himself getting sucked in with unfortunate results. Proceedings took a turn for the worse when in the second episode, as Brent was showing Donna, who was on work experience, the functions of the email system, he discovered a doctored image of himself with his head stuck on the body of a woman in a compromising sexual position with two men.

The usually grinning Brent was seen to be momentarily fazed and, feigning concern that it was offensive to women, he called for an investigation to be immediately mounted by Gareth – putting his Territorial Army covert operations skills to use – to uncover the person responsible. Gareth attempted to pin the blame on Tim, but it was the latter who revealed the real culprit to be David's 'best mate', Chris 'Finchy' Finch. After Jennifer Taylor-Clarke strongly suggested that the prankster be dismissed, the final scene saw Brent appear to call Finch to tell him he'd been fired, until Jennifer switched the speaker phone on to discover that Brent was, in reality, talking to the speaking clock. Such mortifying endings to the episodes became a regular feature of the programme, each surpassing the one before as the degrees of humiliation increased each time.

Viewers who had persevered past the downbeat beginning were rewarded when the third episode nailed the true essence of *The Office*. It centred on the seventh annual Wernham Hogg quiz night, an event which Brent and Finchy – calling themselves, nudge nudge, wink wink, The Dead Parrots – had won consecutively on six previous occasions. Office socials generally bring out the worst in people and this was to be no exception.

Brent's tactlessness was to rear its ugly head once more in a conversation with Tim, who was depressed about reaching his thirtieth birthday. Things could be worse, Brent suggested, Tim could still be living with his parents . . . which he was. Later Dawn and Lee presented Tim with a huge inflatable penis for his birthday, which gave Brent plenty of scope for further lewd comments and the opportunity to show off his misguided sense of humour.

Viewers were also introduced to the foul-mouthed and obnoxious character of the hitherto unseen Chris Finch, who wasted no opportunity in showing up 'best mate' Brent in front of his staff, before making a suggestive remark to Dawn and berating temp Ricky for being a former student.

The quiz night would provide the perfect platform for some more finely observed moments of comedy about male bonding and the male psyche, and how men often act like little boys in grown-up bodies. Predictably, the evening went downhill fast, particularly when The Dead Parrots lost to The Tits (Tim and Ricky), and took defeat very badly.

The fourth episode centred on a staff training day, revealing more absurdity of day-to-day life in the office, and once again Brent excelled himself in showing just how much of a wannabe he was deep down. Having hired a trainer, Rowan, for the day to put staff through a series of exercises, Brent couldn't bear not to be the centre of attention and, despite Rowan's obvious frustration, hogged the spotlight as the staff did role-playing, discussed motivation and watched a training video. (This was directed by Ash Atalla especially for the episode, with ex-*Blue Peter* man Peter Purves – a one-time *Meet Ricky Gervais* guest – dressed in 1980s clothing and sporting dyed hair to give the recording a dated look.)

When Keith expressed a wish to pack in his job and join a band, it prompted Brent to rush home and get his guitar and show off about his old rock'n'roll days, singing some of his own songs including the dreadful 'Free Love Freeway' – obvious echoes here of Gervais's own New Romantic days in Seona Dancing.

In episode five, sexual politics in the workplace became the next subject on *The Office*'s agenda. Donna the work experience girl was the daughter of Brent's close friends and had been staying at his house. However, she had failed to come home on account of having spent the night with Ricky. Her temporary 'guardian' Brent tried to lecture her about her behaviour, but got nowhere and was made to look foolish . . . again.

In spite of the firm's planned cutback, it later transpired that Brent was interviewing for a PA and was shown validating his decision by claiming that taking on another person might even save the company some money long term. Two candidates were interviewed – the first, Stewart Foote (played by Robin Ince), was given short shrift, mainly because he was male, but the second, Karen Roper, looked a more attractive proposition to Brent who hired her on the spot and invited her out with the rest of the office for a celebratory tipple. Afterwards, in a scene of pure slapstick, he managed to headbutt her in the face while fooling around with a football, leaving her reeling.

In a fascinating sequence of male sexual behaviour, later that same evening Finch was seen chatting up a young woman, a reluctant Gareth involved himself in a threesome with a married biker couple, and a frustrated drunken Brent attempted to endear himself to Karen. But one of the most poignant moments of the series so far would see Brent sitting at his desk the next morning reading to camera Sir John Betjeman's famous poem 'Slough', though ironically he didn't mention the fourth verse which makes reference to 'that man with double chin who'll always cheat and always win'.

The image of David Brent as a caring and under-standing boss was quickly punctured at the start of episode six, when he handled the redundancy of a warehouse employee with an appalling lack of profession-alism. Then, when he talked to Tim about why the rep wanted to leave Wernham Hogg to return to university, he quickly became frustrated with Tim's 'whingeing' and told him to get back to work. His self-serving behaviour reached an all-time low when he accepted a promotion that would necessitate the closure of the Slough office.

The scheduled party to mark the end of the financial year went ahead with everyone in low spirits, until Brent announced he had refused his promotion and the Slough branch would remain open after all, merging with the Swindon branch. For once it looked like he'd done the decent thing, but it later transpired that he failed his medical and couldn't take the job.

The series ended with typical flair on a piece of bogus philosophizing and self-promotion from the boss, with a suggestion that the rigours of working life could be made so worthwhile if we all had a boss like David Brent to lighten our load and brighten our working day . . .

What was especially clever about the programme was the way in which it nailed the humdrum nature of white-collar working life. As Gervais told Ed Barrett of spiked-online.com, 'I'm not an anthropologist or sociologist, but I don't think open-plan offices are natural. I imagine that the first thing you do when you're thrown together with thirty people that you might not care for is build a wall.'

Commenting on how they so perfectly captured that atmosphere of boredom, and asked whether he had researched the feeling, Martin Freeman told BBC America, 'No, I didn't. I mean I've only done the research of being bored, the research of having unrequited love, the research of having people annoy the f**k out of me. That was all, really. And I think you can have those experiences whether you're a soldier or a dustman.'

So far, so good, for someone who came into television late in life. 'I was thirty-six when I started work on *The Office*,' Ricky told the *Evening News*. 'Thirty-nine when it was finally broadcast. Sometimes I go, "Oh God! Why didn't I do this ten years ago?" Well, the answer is this. It wouldn't have been as good because a lot of it is based in truth, and draws on my fifteen years working in that environment.'

But Martin Freeman felt the appeal of the series was not solely to do with its being located between four walls. 'To me, the specificity of that *Office* thing is very nice, and very gratifying that people think that. I think it's true we did nail that well, and I'm very proud of it, but I don't think it's specific to an office. I think it's just anyone who's had a working relationship with an idiot boss or a psychotic colleague or fallen in love with someone they shouldn't. I think it's all the research you need really, just to have lived.'

Fortunately for the British viewing public, Ricky Gervais and Stephen Merchant had plenty more to say on the subject, and they wouldn't have to wait too long for the next instalment.

In the meantime, as the last episode of the first series of *The Office* hit the screens in August 2001, Ricky was taking time out at the Edinburgh Fringe Festival, where his show *Rubbernecker* was reaping the rewards of the television series' word-of-mouth popularity. 'It's me and three mates who decided to go up to Edinburgh together for a laugh,' he told the *Sunday Herald*, claiming their eight-day stint had occurred at the last moment 'because a venue fell free and we only decided the day before that we'd do it. It's not like we want to win the Perrier [award] or anything.'

The show was advertised as follows: 'Comics messing about and possibly embarrassing themselves. The title? There'll be bits you know you shouldn't watch, but be compelled to, in the same way as a car crash.'

Ricky's three friends were Stephen Merchant, inevitably, plus *11 O'Clock Show* writers Jimmy Carr and Robin Ince. It wasn't Merchant's first time at the Fringe. In his last year at Warwick, while still an ambitious stand-up, he went up to Edinburgh and took part in a sketch show. 'We performed to about eight people,' he said. 'It was not an enormous financial or critical success. But it was great fun.'

Gervais had only visited the festival as a spectator when he was entertainments manager for ULU, but regarded his performing debut with equanimity. 'I don't do stand-up so I don't have all these clever put-downs like, "Mate, shut up or I'll stab you." But why would they heckle when I'm on? If they start, I'll just introduce the next turn and go off: "Jimmy Carr said you were a bunch of wankers, and he was right. So here he is!"

'I've done about five gigs, and people laughed because they recognized me off the telly. I found them easy, which means I must have been doing something wrong, because stand-up is really difficult.' He admitted that he was still learning the ropes regarding stand-up and had been surprised to hear that 'Comedians never have a drink before they go on. I had to find that out.'

The new show, in retrospect, was the forerunner of Ricky's later podcasts, and he admitted he had doubts about its improvised nature when he found out tickets were selling like hot cakes. 'I started feeling a bit sorry for the people who've paid ten quid to come along and see four idiots make it up,' he told Graeme Virtue of the *Sunday Herald*. 'I feel we should give them something back, so I have started to think about it.

'Basically,' he continued, 'the three others have got a nice routine each and I'm going to compere it in the style of an arrogant, D-list celebrity who thinks he's famous now and these three are on his shirt-tails. It's a character of mine that gets on telly a bit – he's been on *Night Fever* and he knows most of the cast of *The Bill* – and he really thinks he's made it now.'

His character was Derek, whose childlike innocence, mixed with a reality-TV-fuelled lust for fame, was a combination designed to be positively aggravating. 'He hasn't grown up. It's an excuse to see the world differently. It's not meant to be a piss-take of the retarded or whatever . . . He'll do anything to get somewhere,' Gervais explained.

Ricky described Jimmy Carr's character as 'an uptight middle-class bloke, but there's something quite clever about him. He does a lot of surreal one-liners – like Emo Philips but in a Radio 4 English panel-game-type way. Robin [Ince] is a lot more free-form, a lot more like classic stand-up, like rambling Ross Noble. He's a bit of a loser – again, that's the character! Steve Merchant hasn't actually got any jokes but he doesn't need any. He's six foot seven with a face like some sort of strange thing.'

The act 'sort of evolved', he explained in *Scotland on Sunday,* 'and it changes every time we speak to each other. Originally, it was very free-form. Now it's developed into four people doing their own thing and we've got to do eighteen minutes each. I don't know what it is really. It's four separate people doing vaguely stand-up stuff. That's it. I haven't sold that very well, have I?'

Reviews were universally favourable. 'The only disappointment about *Rubbernecker* is its all too brief run,' said *The Herald,* adding, 'You'll be aching for more,' while *The List* thought the comedians 'a brilliant mix – their styles complement each other incredibly well'.

Ince and Gervais reprised their double act in a series of 2001 Christmas and New Year ads for the video music channel MTV. A typecast Ricky starred as what *Creative Review* magazine described as 'a socially inadequate, lonely record shop owner, struggling to have something resembling a life'. Gervais insisted on keeping the shop open on Christmas Day, playing a lonely game of pass the parcel with assistant Ince, and visiting Ricky's flat upstairs where, it became clear, his mother also lived. The tableau was enlivened by visits from MTV presenters Zane Lowe and Natalie Casey plus Boyzone's Ronan Keating. Director Deborah Woolfe revealed that Keating (who is greeted as a member of the Backstreet Boys) had not originally seen the funny side of Ricky's script. 'He was a little sceptical at first, but then he really got into it.'

Soon it was time to get back to more serious business, because Ricky and Stephen had to satisfy an *Office* audience that was clearly hungry for more.

6

—

Encores and Awards

❝ Ideas are what matter to me, they're the thing that keeps me going – not the awards, not even the ratings. We wouldn't want to come back for a half-hearted encore . . . ❞

DESPITE ITS relatively low ratings, there was no hesitation on BBC2's part to commission a second series of *The Office* – and the show proved its worth when it won Best New Comedy at the British Comedy Awards in December 2001. The BBC channel also took the unprecedented step of a quick repeat in January 2002, and the re-run actually saw an increase in figures. Three months later *The Office* won the first of six BAFTAs for Best Comedy Performance for Ricky and Best Sitcom. The second series followed pretty swiftly, coming to the screen on 30 September 2002, and gaining a startlingly high figure (in comparison to the first) of 5.2 million.

The writing partnership of Gervais and Merchant had been an unmitigated success, but although the basis of their relationship was very much one of equals, it was Merchant who came across as the one in the adult role. 'The only thing we argue about,' says Stephen, 'is where to go for lunch. Ricky has the palate of a seven-year-old – he's like one of those kids Jamie Oliver was trying to re-educate.' He certainly disputes any similarity between his writing partner and David Brent. 'They're polar opposites,' he told the *Sunday Express* in 2002. 'Ricky is concerned with doing the right thing, while David is only ever interested in number one. The only similarity is that they're both work-shy, jowly and have dubious facial hair.'

During the course of their *Office* experience, the pair got so used to working together that Merchant admits he now finds it very hard to write material without using Ricky as a sounding board. 'I can't judge if something's funny on my own.'

Gervais says the single most important aspect of their partnership is empathy. 'Empathy is the most important thing in life. It's the point of life. So many people forget that.' Hence nothing ever goes in one of their creations that they both don't like. Anything that's left over goes in Ricky's live show, 'so nothing's wasted. We only need do two minutes of TV a day – that's about two or three pages [of script]. We never let anyone give us deadlines. If we want to take two years doing two hours a day or one year doing four hours a day, that's what we'll do,' he explained to *Time Out*'s Graham Wray.

When the BBC finally allocated them a room where they could write *The Office* script, Stephen claims he had to keep it completely empty to prevent Ricky from getting distracted. 'We borrowed someone's office because we couldn't work at [Ricky's] house any more: there were too many distractions,' he revealed to Bruce Dessau. 'He's got toys, animals, bright lights, mirrors. Anything will distract him. So we asked the BBC if we could have an office, and we used to sneak into people's offices when they weren't there.'

One day, after a heavy lunch, Ricky decided to lie on the floor under Stephen's desk. 'I did some typing, and occasionally I'd ask some questions, and he'd snore or mumble something. And I was acting out a scene we'd written, and reading it back for him. I knocked on the desk, and he leapt up, thinking someone had come in. He didn't want to get caught looking work-shy . . .'

Ricky prefers to describe himself as the more mobile half of the partnership. 'It's me who walks round the room eating biscuits and Steve who has to transcribe it,' he told *Time Out* magazine. 'We have a framework and talk about what we might fill it with for ages. It's usually from observations. You never know what you're going to come up with, so from 11 a.m. to 3 p.m. we just sit there. It might be an hour of telling stories about when you were a kid, or what we saw on the tube coming in, and then *bang* . . .'

The pair find that many of their ideas come from just talking about friends' experiences. Of every eight hours he and Merchant spend working on scripts, 'six will be spent talking about films, what worked and what didn't'. In terms of their ideas, it pays to have a good memory because Ricky refuses to carry a Dictaphone around with him or write anything down between meetings. He thinks that 'over the last twenty years I've lost two sitcoms and four stand-up shows'. He subscribes to the Woody Allen dictum: 'The best an idea gets is when it's in your head. From then on, it's just a matter of how much you ruin it.'

Back in *The Office*, if viewers were beginning to believe that the thick-skinned Brent was a cat with nine lives, season two would introduce a more solemn tone. Changes in the management structure meant that Brent was now a man out on a limb. The new series explored his insecurities, rivalries and petty jealousies, giving *The Office* more edge and tension than the first series had – David B. was now a man under siege.

The new season opened two weeks after the first one had ended, and reorganization was in the air as the two branches of Wernham Hogg merged. New regional boss Neil Godwin was scheduled to talk to the staff alongside Jennifer. His well-received presentation stung the once cocky, now insecure Brent to the bone. At a drinks reception afterwards Brent jealously attempted to gain the attention of the ex-Swindon employees with a racist joke Gareth had told earlier. It immediately caused offence with certain staff members and culminated in a severe reprimand for the hapless manager.

The second show revolved around staff appraisals and there were telling interviews with Gareth, Tim, Big Keith and Dawn, the latter revealing she still nursed hopes of becoming a children's illustrator. Inevitably, though, the episode returned to the now-simmering rivalry between Brent and Neil, which erupted when one of the new-comers from the Swindon branch confided to Brent that there wasn't much 'dynamism' in the Slough office and that staff were getting away with murder. A shocked Brent asked the Swindon lot how many of them thought that Neil was more of a laugh than he was, and was gutted when confronted with a sea of hands indicating the affirmative. The show ended with a shaken Brent confiding his feelings to Dawn, but taking solace when she reassured him that he was, indeed, funnier than Neil.

The issue of disability was also key to this episode. It was a subject that Gervais has never shied away from, both during his time on *The 11 O'Clock Show* and in his stand-up, his love of jokes about disability first featured in *The Office* in the first series, with a crack about Stephen Hawking's football boots; indeed a couple of years later the comedian would describe the wheelchair-bound genius as 'lazy' at an awards ceremony.

In the second series, this disability fixation would eventually reach a peak in the second episode, when, during a fire drill, Brent and Gareth decided to leave wheelchair-user Brenda halfway down the stairwell. Brenda, who had joined the Slough office from Swindon, was also the focus of a typically un-PC email from Brent, which appeared in *The Office: The Scripts, Series 2* book. In it he explained that all the staff had been informed of her 'condition' in order to be better prepared for her arrival. He also revealed that a ramp had been installed, and, in a bizarre attempt to reassure her, mentioned that someone in accounts was a volunteer worker with Down's syndrome people . . .

Some took exception to this form of humour, finding it both tasteless and bigoted, but it was an obsession that was to become a staple of Gervais's act. Many felt that he had overstepped the mark on the night of the annual British Comedy Awards in 2001 when, accompanied by his wheelchair-using producer Ash Atalla, Gervais decided to 'run the risk of offending everyone in the country' by making fun of Ash's disability.

'Aah, look at his little face,' said Gervais, beaming, before adding that Ash 'wants to make it clear that he is not a competition winner'. While Atalla responded with a 'wanker' hand gesture, there was an ominous pause from the audience before they broke into laughter. The long-suffering producer took the quip in his stride, commenting to *The Independent Magazine,* 'I've worked with Ricky for four years and he's still more obsessed by my wheelchair than anyone else I know.'

Down but not out, an obviously rattled David Brent arrived late at the start of the third episode sporting a cheap version of Neil's Armani leather jacket, boasting that he didn't need fashionable clothes to be cool and 'rock'n'roll'. His fortunes appeared to have changed when two reps from consultancy firm Cooper and Webb arrived to ask him to take part in a management training session for which he would be paid £300 for fifteen minutes' work.

Brent's feelings of jealousy soon resurfaced, though, at a champagne and cake party for Trudy's birthday, especially when it became apparent that Neil had master-minded the whole event. He became even more incensed by the relaxed repartee between Neil and Finchy, who gave each other a secret handshake. The episode ended with Brent facing total humiliation when his attempt to compete with Neil and Finchy's jokes went too far and had him graphically miming simulated sex with the female members of Irish group The Corrs while his staff looked on in abject horror.

It was Brent's big day as a 'motivational speaker' in the

next programme, but first there were a couple of nasty home truths he had to handle. It was quickly becoming apparent that the seemingly unruffled, happy-go-lucky manager from the first series was now history. Far from being regarded as the perfect boss, he discovered that the Swindon staff had uncomplimentary names for him like Bluto (from the *Popeye* cartoon) and Mr Toad, 'the ugliest of all the amphibians'. To make matters worse, some of the new staff had yet to be paid, which was purely down to Brent, and because it was not the first time he had forgotten something important, he faced an angry reprimand from Neil for his shoddy methods.

With storm clouds on the horizon, Brent and Dawn went off to the community centre to do his presentation, Brent cutting a ludicrous figure in 'expert speaker gear' of basketball cap, jeans and T-shirt. The lecture didn't go any better – having opened his talk with an aggressive 'Get out', Brent continued by quoting a maxim from a book of *Collected Meditations* and interpreting it in his uniquely nonsensical style, before jumping around to the strains of Tina Turner's 'Simply the Best' and leaving behind a stunned audience.

The penultimate show of the second series offered a mixture of high comedy and real pathos. Red Nose Day at Wernham Hogg was bound to provide a platform for Brent to indulge in his usual silly behaviour – he got to don a red nose and also get inside an ostrich costume – but the ultimate highlight was the irrefutably bad dance routine he indulged in after Neil and Rachel's *Saturday Night Fever* pastiche. It has since become one of those classic comedy moments of TV history, like Basil Fawlty thrashing his car with the branch of a tree.

Talking of it in retrospect to *Time Out* magazine, Gervais has admitted, 'I nearly didn't put the dance in. I think I was probably annoying Steve one day, doing the dance while he wanted to work. I annoy people for a living but, you see, it's never wasted. So we said a fat forty-year-old trying to dance cool is funny, but not funny enough, so how do we justify it? It took five seconds to write "Ricky does a funny dance" but it was all the stuff working back from it that took the time.

'Why has he done that dance? Because he's jealous of Neil. Why is he jealous? 'Cos Neil's done this choreographed and rehearsed dance because it's his party piece every Red Nose Day. But this is Brent's favourite day of the year. So suddenly it resonates, it feels organic and natural, and you don't see the join.'

Featuring a cameo appearance from Stephen Merchant as Oggy, aka the Oggmonster, the show would end on a dark note, with Jennifer and Neil admonishing Brent for his negligence and a hurt Brent challenging his new boss to sack him. Although it had been a throwaway remark, his bluff was well and truly called when he was later offered a surprise redundancy package. This perfectly set up a final episode, which opened with Brent trying to put on a brave face to camera about his imminent departure.

With a tone now less arrogant and laced with bravado and not a little desperation, Brent blithely compared his situation to the one faced by Jesus – how the son of God hadn't rested on his laurels or only half completed his mission to spread the word. While he was keen to point out that his world didn't end in Slough, rather than taking a more national or global view of places where he could move on to, he reeled off a list of cities and towns solely in the local area, proving once and for all that his goals were limited, his aspirations decidedly under-whelming.

A hoped-for graceful swansong, a profile for trade magazine *Inside Paper,* was not to be either. Despite trying to write his own copy, the interview was sabotaged by a series of unfortunate events, firstly by Dawn coming in to tender her own resignation and then the arrival of the reps from Cooper and Webb to tell him no more motivational speeches would be required.

For a programme that initially wallowed in its low-key approach, the end of the series wrung some serious emotion out of the situation as Neil and Jennifer went through the details of Brent's redundancy. When Neil extended his hand to an almost broken Brent, the latter took it and wouldn't let go, begging his superiors to reconsider and earnestly assuring them he would change his ways and try harder.

But of course the series had to go out with just one more piece of priceless cod philosophizing to camera. It was to be one of Brent's finest, as unintentionally funny as anything he'd come up with during the previous eleven episodes. Referring to the highs and lows of the daily grind, and the unpredictability of everyday life, he rounded off his musings with the thought-provoking quotation: 'If you want the rainbow, you've got to put up with the rain.' After revealing the originator of the maxim to be none other than Dolly Parton, he leaves the viewer to absorb this detail for a split second before closing with, 'and people say she's just a big pair of tits . . .'

The show always seemed to have a moral subtext – and this was especially true of the love triangle between Dawn, Tim and Lee. It was developed slowly and subtly over the course of the twelve episodes, starting with occasional flirtatious exchanges and building to a more obvious expression of romance in the fourth episode when Tim first comforted her after an argument with Lee and then asked her out, not knowing that in the meantime the pair had made up.

From then on in until the final episode, the camera discreetly captured the ups and downs between the pair, from Dawn's occasional lingering look across the office in Tim's direction to the thaw in relations at the start of the second series when they jokily danced together and a jealous Lee pushed Tim out the way. Despite a romance with newcomer Rachel, Tim continued to be interested in Dawn, only to be rebuffed a second time.

Viewers were left disappointed when Dawn decided to go off to Florida to start a new life with Lee, despite her feelings for Tim. And the unfinished affair between the pair played no small part in the commissioning of two Christmas specials.

Asked why she didn't leave Lee for Tim, actress Lucy Davis told BBC America: 'I think that the torturous thing was that if Tim had asked Dawn a week before she would have probably said yes. But when he asked her she had already organized the whole Florida trip. I think that it was just too big a thing for her to go "Yes" to Tim and, "Oh, by the way, Lee. Cancel the flights. Cancel your life." She was too far in, and I think he was just a bit late.'

By 2003, after the broadcast of the second series,

which saw it cross over into mainstream entertainment and the minds and hearts of the nation, *The Office* had become just about the biggest phenomenon on terrestrial TV. It even produced a docu-soap spin-off about a car-hire firm in Swansea, *The Real Life of The Office*. According to press reports, however, Ricky's brother Larry was less than taken with the critically acclaimed programme. Although he acknowledged that it was 'beautifully written', he explained that he found it 'absolutely painful to watch and really not very funny. I feel obliged to watch it, but just now I'm not a fan.'

Despite his brother's reservations, Ricky Gervais had become media personality of the year, and the subject of endless interviews. He was, however, heartened that both the public and the media had stuck with the show. 'I'm surprised I didn't get the backlash for the second series of *The Office*,' he told *Future Movies*. 'In America the more you achieve the more they like you, in England it's like, "Now he's getting too big for his boots" – we love the underdog and when they win, they're not the underdog anymore.'

He was no longer just another wannabe from Reading and had become fiercely outspoken about his baby: 'At no point in the life of *The Office* has it never been a spoof documentary,' he informed *The Independent Magazine*. 'It's been a false documentary – not so much faking a genre, but because we wanted you to watch it as if David Brent was real, and that seemed the best way to do it.

'We liked the fact that he is a normal person who, when given his platform, he thinks, This is it, I'm a philosopher, I'm the next [*Cruise* star] Jane McDonald . . . but he opens his mouth and blows it. When someone says, "You should meet Ted, he's the funniest bloke you'll ever meet," I can guarantee you that he won't be – he'll come up with one of those buzzer things in his hand and you'll go, "Isn't he great?"'

Quizzed as to the dividing line between comic character and real life, he told *The Observer*, 'By definition you can't know, but I don't think I've got a huge blind spot. I don't think I'm going through a mid-life crisis, and I don't go up to black people and ask them about rap.' He also revealed that he consciously changed the way he spoke when in character: 'I exaggerated a bit. I went a little more Reading with Brent, and I also tried to slow it down so he . . . is . . . more . . . professional . . . than me.'

Still speaking of Brent, he further elaborated to Ed Barrett, 'Well, he's that part of all us that wants to be liked and thought of as a good bloke, and also wants desperately to win at Trivial Pursuit. Most of us manage to keep it under control, though.

'David Brent's not a bad bloke, but he's full of contradictions. Part of him regrets missing out on the 1980s, and thinks he could have had his own business now and owned a Maserati by now. But he also wants this California thing – a big commune. He doesn't know if he wants to be the head of the Mafia or a guru. He wants to win, but if he was a bit more honest and vulnerable, and occasionally admitted he was having a bad day, people would like him more.'

In *The Observer* Gervais explained how he perfected the character of Brent and how he managed such a frighteningly real portrayal of this delusional manager in mid-life crisis: 'I was a couch comedy philosopher. I knew that it was all about the rendering. When I wrote *The*

Office I had a much bigger list of don'ts than dos. I knew that people didn't talk in poetic prose. I knew that people didn't always end with a punchline – there was an aftermath. I knew that people didn't talk in funny voices, that awful Oxbridge tradition. And I hated exposition. There are no comedy gimmicks with David Brent. Therefore I knew at the time of making *The Office* that he could come back to haunt me. But you know I couldn't give a f**k!'

It wasn't surprising that Gervais drew on his own real-life experiences for *The Office*. There were scenes taken directly from his early years, such as the moment in the very first episode where Brent interviewed an applicant for the job of forklift-truck operator while telling lies to his warehouse manager on the phone. This was based on something that had actually happened to Ricky when, as a school leaver, he'd applied for work via a recruitment agency.

The man who interviewed him phoned a friend and lied in order to get Gervais a job; as he did so, he winked and made a Pinocchio-type nose with his hand. 'This guy was supposed to be his mate,' Gervais told Ed Barrett, 'and I was meant to be impressed by this man lying to a friend! It's the arrogance of people who meet someone and want to take the short cut. They go, "I'll be honest – you're going to like me because everyone else does, so let's cut the bullshit and start liking me now."'

The video/DVD sales for both series of *The Office* was a phenomenon in itself: series one would go on to sell over one million copies, while the second series sold some 143,000 copies on DVD alone in the first month of its release in October 2003. Not at all bad for a pair of 'total chancers', as Ricky once described Merchant and himself.

The impact *The Office* had made on mainstream television and life in general became apparent when, in January 2004, its opening credit sequence was recreated to introduce the BBC's flagship discussion show *Question Time*, which was being hosted in Slough. Not only that, but Gervais had been asked to appear on the panel (an invitation he had politely declined).

Independent councillor Tony Haines declared himself unhappy with the 'sort of stereotypical image of Slough' represented by *The Office* and, by association, *Question Time*. He'd been even more upset fifteen months earlier when council bosses publicly admitted they wanted to hire Ricky as Slough's cultural ambassador in the week they announced plans to close five play-centres and axe scores of jobs. Wisely, Gervais had again turned down the offer.

Two years and a number of awards would change any negative perceptions *The Office* had brought with it, to the extent that by 2006 Slough would be positively basking in the association. Richard Paxton, centre manager of the Queensmere shopping centre, said: '*The Office* has helped to encourage a positive image of Slough, and I would encourage any tourist coming to Slough because of the show. It is excellent for the town and hopefully it will be good for business.'

Councillor George Davidson, the council's deputy leader, was of the opinion that everyone should enjoy the fact that the show is based in Slough, adding hopefully: 'Ricky Gervais is a local lad, so when he thought where to set *The Office* he picked a town which would be realistic because it has the best job and employment opportunities in the south-east.' And council leader Rob Anderson – not the man behind the 'cultural ambassador' stunt – said: 'All publicity is good publicity. There are worse things to be associated with than an iconic comedy series. We can roll with the punches.'

Gervais himself claimed there'd been no malice aforethought in his choice of location. 'Why Slough?' he mused to *Q* magazine in 2002. 'Apart from it being onomatopoeic – Slooough – we wanted somewhere very ordinary and unglamorous. Not that I know – I've only been there once when I was a kid. It probably has changed.' Slough, halfway between Reading and London, had a reason for being notoriously prickly as to how it was portrayed. It had been a byword for mediocrity since it was the subject of Betjeman's poem some sixty-five years previously. 'Come friendly bombs and fall on Slough/It isn't fit for humans now,' wrote the future Poet Laureate, prompting lasting ridicule for the town's inhabitants.

The Independent elicited the last word from Gervais on the siting of his first big hit in September 2002. 'If I opened fêtes I wouldn't turn down Slough,' he said, before adding significantly, 'it's the opening fêtes bit I'd turn down. It seems I'm turning down offers every day. It's not a reflection on the quality of the offers, more that I'm sick of the sight of me. I don't want to piss the public off by popping up on things. I think I've got a really limited shelf life and I want to spread that out over the next five years.'

The Office would go on to win a cupboardful of awards in 2002, the first of which came in February when veteran comedian Norman Wisdom presented Ricky with *The South Bank Show* Comedy Award. Respected writer Richard Curtis, best known for *Blackadder* and *The Vicar of Dibley*, as well as hit films *Four Weddings and a Funeral* and *Notting Hill*, was moved to rate *The Office* 'the best funny TV [I've] probably ever seen' when picking up an award of his own.

After winning two BAFTAs in April, the Royal Television Society Programme Awards later that year saw *The Office* beat off competition from Chris Morris's controversial *Brass Eye* special on paedophiles and Peter Kay's *Phoenix Nights* to take the award for Best Situation Comedy and Comedy Drama. Ricky, who was also nominated for the Best Actor prize but lost to David Suchet, accepted the award but left the stage saying nothing. In contrast, comic Johnny Vegas spent longer at the microphone than anyone else and even offered to stay and help Graham Norton host the rest of the show!

The annual Broadcasting Press Guild awards brought another pair of prizes in 2002 when *The Office* was named Best Entertainment Show, and Ricky and Stephen also won the Writer's Award. The latter particularly pleased Ricky, who broke his customary shy silence to say: 'I am pleased the writing has been recognized, because that is the most important thing in comedy or drama. It is not high concept, or art, it is just a telly programme, but the exciting thing is coming up with ideas and thinking, "I'm going to see this on the telly."'

Nevertheless, even after a second successful series of *The Office* – like *Fawlty Towers*, he elected to stop at two – Ricky felt a downward arc to his career was looming. Revealing his fears to the *Daily Record*, he opined: 'When

I wrote the first series, I was surrounded by ten years of ideas, and I couldn't have written them quickly enough. Second time round I found it easier because I'd become a better actor, director and writer.

'But there's more pressure this time round because the show is a success. People took it on board because they felt they had discovered it themselves. It was new, which it isn't now; it captured a zeitgeist, which it can't now; and we were the underdogs, which we're not now. Looks as if it's downhill from here, doesn't it? I suppose I'd better chuck it all in.'

One judge whose opinion Ricky valued was to be found at home in the shape of Jane Fallon. 'We always sit down and watch the programme together,' she revealed to the *Daily Mirror*. 'I will laugh away like a maniac, and then Ricky will point out something that didn't quite work, which is annoying because you're happily watching it. He gives a bit of a running commentary and he'll laugh at Tim or Gareth but not at himself.'

Clearly, he was his own greatest critic.

7

The Science of Success

❦ My career path? Ten years working towards being a scientist, and then ten doing music, and then two or three doing comedy; I could still end up being Gary Barlow. ❧

THE SUCCESS of *The Office*, thanks to word-of-mouth support bolstered by repeats and DVD issues, made Ricky Gervais a man very much in demand. But most of what that entailed didn't meet with his approval. 'I avoid showbiz parties, don't go up the red carpet, and don't like talking about myself much,' he explained to the *Evening News*. 'I'll talk about *The Office* until the cows come home, but I won't tell where I shop, or who I'm supporting for the FA Cup.'

In the run-up to the 2002 general election, he was indulging in his time-honoured weekly pleasure of reading the *New Musical Express*, and was disgusted with what he found. 'They'd print which pop stars were voting Labour and who supported the Conservatives and I'd think, "Why do I care who [teen singer] Billie is going to vote for?"' It all strengthened his resolve not to be 'a pundit'. But it was impossible to resist every invitation . . .

When you're famous, you can expect to be targeted by one of two broadcasting institutions – TV's *This Is Your Life* or radio's *Desert Island Discs*. With the Big Red Book safely out of commission and Michael Aspel's time occupied with *The Antiques Roadshow*, Ricky probably thought the odds were in his favour. But in April 2002 he was to fall victim to a somewhat newer celebrity TV showcase – BBC2's *Room 101*.

Hosted by comic Paul Merton, it invited the rich and famous to rid their world of things that caused them grief, aggravation, annoyance or any combination thereof. Perhaps it was the fact that he was facing another funnyman, maybe it was his usual slightly shifty small-screen demeanour, but Ricky seemed ill at ease as he became the last celeb of the series to reveal his wish list.

He'd later confess to having treated his appearance as a role-playing exercise. 'That was closer to me than David Brent or *Meet Ricky Gervais*,' he conceded in a *Scotland on Sunday* interview, 'but there is still some persona in there. You are still performing a little bit. I had to choose things to go in *Room 101* that I had a bit of comedy on. I didn't just want to reel off a list: spiders, cancer, you know what I mean.'

There were definite echoes of *The Office* in Ricky's 'performance'. His obsequious laughter at Merton's jokes recalled Brent doing likewise to 'Finchy', while he recycled another Brent line when he prefaced his blue jokes with a warning that 'you'll have to cut this'.

The first object of his good-natured wrath, as befitted a non-parent by choice, was people who take their babies/toddlers to restaurants. This was followed by the offence of lateness and people who make unnecessary noises. When it came to tardiness, not even a bereavement was a good enough excuse – 'Well, you knew she was ill. Plan ahead!' – while the purgatory of caravan holidays took him back to his youth.

The closest he came to anything too personal or seriously nasty was when he nominated Children In Need or similar charity telethons that 'render the whole nation into a giant rag week'. As it turns out, it was celebrities like Lesley Joseph, *Birds of a Feather*'s Dorien, who did a belly dance, and Dawn French and Robbie Coltrane – 'Do we really need *them* telling us there is not enough food?' – he attacked rather than the events themselves.

As the interrogation continued, there were signs that the one-time host of *Meet Ricky Gervais* was beginning to hold his own, directing the conversation as he pleased. But the tables were neatly turned when host Merton played a clip of Seona Dancing from 1983, leaving Ricky somewhat embarrassed. According to one viewer: 'Gervais blushed inside his heavy suit . . . and Merton did nothing to help. "What was the name of the band?" he finally asked. Ricky mumbled something unintelligible. More silence. Said Merton, wickedly: "Want to say anything else about that?" It was like watching something boil in a bag . . .'

Less traumatic have been his numerous TV appearances on *Friday Night with Jonathan Ross*. First invited on to the programme in November 2002, his boisterous banter with friend and host Ross has been a regular highlight of the show. Outside of 'work' the two men have often been spotted dining out together with their partners (the two Janes – Fallon and Goldman), and they also enjoy a healthy rivalry with regard to their radio shows (on Radio 2 and Xfm respectively), as both have been nominated for the same awards over the past few years. They were even rumoured to be working on a joint comedy venture in March 2003, when it was reported that they were filming a pilot for a new programme at MTV studios. Their collaboration came to nothing, however, as the show was never broadcast.

The success of *The Office* and the many awards it brought in its wake would turn the spotlight on Ricky like never before. And, to put it mildly, he didn't look comfortable with it. 'I just hate the celebrity thing,' he moaned to the *Mirror.* 'While I'm pleased to win all these awards, I find it embarrassing. I'd rather not go, but then people will think, "He is so arrogant. He's been on the TV for two minutes and he thinks he's Woody Allen." I'd rather be down the pub with my friends.'

The tabloid 'celebrity' interviews with superficial questions like 'What is your favourite colour?' were one thing, the 'in-depths' for the likes of *The Guardian* and the Sunday 'heavies' another. He tended to play the celebrity interviewers along for their very literality. When asked what three things he'd rescue if his house caught fire, Ricky came up with his cat, his salamander and, when he couldn't think of anything else, 'one of the twins'. Some months later, another celebrity interviewer who'd clearly done her research, asked how old his twins were . . .

Something that Ricky might have been glad not to have to justify in interviews was his cameo appearance as a doorman in the December 2001 film release *Dog Eat Dog*. Directed and written by Moody Shoaibi, it was described by *Total Film* magazine as 'a sloppily edited sequence of unfunny episodes involving four west London-based DJ friends who ... incur the wrath of a local drug dealer'. Its roll-call of guest stars also included Gary Kemp, Alan Davies and All Saints' Melanie Blatt. 'Less dogs, more bollocks, it's facile, juvenile and completely missable,' *Total Film* concluded.

Given the unerring nature of his own characterizations, Ricky, who delivered all of three lines, would undoubtedly have agreed with another reviewer who pointed out that the film was 'too busy trying to be cool and hip that it forgets the most important thing about low-budget comedy: character!'

The opportunities open to Ricky to make the most of *The Office*'s success came thick and fast – and in April 2002, *The Daily Telegraph* reported that high-street electrical retailer Dixons had employed him to make a staff training video. The intention was that store workers looked on Ricky's performance with samples of the shop's photographic range as 'a great demonstration of what not to do'. There was clearly a publicity value to this, as a spokesman confirmed. 'From now on, Dixons staff will be trained by Dave [*sic*] Brent. A consultancy pitched the idea at us, and we thought he would be able to inject a bit of humour into the programme.'

At the time, Gervais appeared justifiably proud of himself, telling reporter Guy Adams, with tongue in cheek, that he was 'delighted to do it. After all, I am following in the footsteps of Graham Norton and Davina McCall.' This attitude would soon be replaced by a more discerning policy, to the extent that only charities are now likely to succeed in obtaining his services.

Seven months later, David Brent emerged from *The Office* once again for a rare moment of freedom. Ricky had agreed to lend him to an ad campaign to encourage more disabled people into employment, waiving his fee and encouraging *The Office*'s production crew to work for nothing on a commercial which was screened in cinemas the following month.

Brent trod the shop floor as the foreman of an engineering works who embodied every preconception going with regards to disabled people. Asked by an unseen interviewer if he would employ a disabled person, Brent replies that he would – but not dwarves 'because they would want to take a lot of time off, especially during the panto season', and not anybody in a wheelchair 'because they knock stuff over'.

The initiative cleverly tied in with the fact that the second series of *The Office* had featured a disabled character. Ad agency creative director Robert Jebb produced a skeleton script, which Gervais agreed to develop and produce. 'Comedy is what I do, and it's also a powerful tool for a serious message,' Gervais said. 'Sadly, there's a bit of us all reflected in Brent and that's the point.'

Interviewed by advertising trade magazine *Campaign*, Jebb acknowledged that the commercial might be thought insulting and insensitive by some people. But he added: 'Anybody without a disability should take a long, hard look at it because it does a good job for a good cause. There will always be some disabled people who are upset by it, but we think we've done this in a way that cares and supports.'

By now, it was more than apparent that Ricky Gervais was not able to accept the pressures of stardom with any kind of ease. He began to take the double precaution of wearing headphones on trains and burying his head in a book to discourage conversation, while his passage around the Bloomsbury area was at a fast clip with head down and gaze averted.

Combine that with the physical attributes of a man in the throes of early middle age, and his decision to participate in a televised charity boxing bout in December 2002 appears even less explicable. Grant Bovey, the businessman husband of TV presenter Anthea Turner, was the opponent he was selected to face on BBC2's *The Fight Over Christmas* – surely a Channel 4 programme in the wrong place.

Yet apart from having champion heavyweight Muhammad Ali as his all-time hero, there seemed little else Gervais could point to in his favour. 'I did a bit of karate years ago and I've punched a bag, but that's about it,' he told the *Radio Times*.

Furthermore, he couldn't pinpoint his motivation. 'I turn down two or three celebrity things a day. I don't like doing it. I can't think what possessed me to say yes to the worst one possible.'

He'd never taken part in a boxing match before, 'because I thought I'd lose my looks, but now I've got nothing left to lose. Boxing is barbaric . . . but it's very exciting and I've got a lot of respect for anyone who'd put themselves through that.'

Comics Bob Mortimer and Les Dennis had subjected themselves to a similar ordeal earlier that year for TV's *Sport Relief.* Gervais had seen them and thought 'two middle-aged men flailing around a room, a bit flabby and panting, doing windmill punches, then running away and quietly vomiting' was a somewhat sad spectacle. But since he was 'sort of starting to get fit anyway [in] the last few months' he decided to accept the invitation. 'If I said I was wholly doing it for charity then I'd be lying.' Even so, he admitted that, 'For the first and hopefully the last time in my life, I've out-stupided David Brent.'

His nutritionist had advised him that he was taking in too many carbohydrates, so the usual Gervais diet was replaced by green vegetables 'and protein like fish, ham and nuts. I've got to eat more often, too – usually I have a big lunch and a big dinner and skip breakfast.' Ricky actually put on weight over the month 'because the nutritionist said I could eat an extra meal a day'.

His opponent was roughly the same age and weight, though taller and with a greater reach, 'so I've got to learn to slip inside his jab. I don't know Grant at all, so it's not a grudge match.'

Four weeks of daily training at the Fight Factory gym on London's Old Kent Road began embarrassingly. Owner Eugene Maloney recalled: 'The first time we put him in the ring he got punched on the nose and dropped to the floor.' Later sparring partners included

Bob Mortimer, who he quickly sent to the canvas . . . apologizing all the while! 'I got him a beauty and he went down and I was saying, "Oh, sorry!" and my corner were screaming, "Don't f**king apologize."' But he was in peak form when, clad in a flowing red cape and matching red shorts, he finally entered the ring at the BBC Television Centre with 'Granite' Grant.

Bovey had became something of a national punchbag when he walked out on his family for Anthea – and, in a move some claimed was straight out of the David Brent training manual, Ricky reportedly proclaimed his plan to have his opponent's ex-wife Della in his corner! That didn't happen, of course, but real blood was spilled in the three ninety-second rounds that followed the opening bell.

Grant pushed Ricky over and then he got his own back by pushing Grant over, 'like kids in the playground . . . We threw punches and locked and then went mental.' Ricky found the contest to be gruelling and exhausting, concluding, 'It's the worst experience I've ever been through . . . It was harder, more painful than anything that's ever happened to me. And I was more knackered than I've ever been.'

He admitted the fight was by some way 'the most violent thing I've ever been through. I knew I couldn't stop – the worrying thing was I would have carried on if I'd had a heart attack or got a fractured skull.' It was the kind of thing he'd have used his wit to avoid at Ashmead Comprehensive. But having pledged the £5,000 purse to his chosen charity, Macmillan cancer nurses, he was in no position to throw in the towel.

His girlfriend Jane was in the audience, along with

several cast members from *The Office*. 'First they were excited, then they realized it was a proper fight, and then it was, "Oh, God! He's getting hit." Then afterwards they thought maybe I was brain damaged. I think Jane knew it was going to be safe. I think she was worried, but she cheered up when I was doing well.'

Ricky won the first round, but Grant levelled in the second. 'He got me in the rib and I couldn't sleep for days. During the fight I was thinking, Right, he's done a rib, but I can still breathe. It's amazing what adrenalin and fear of losing in front of people will do. By the third round, we were both just walking wounded. I threw lots of combination punches to try to impress the judges.'

Ricky won the final round and the match, but revealed: 'It didn't matter that I'd won. I just wanted to go home. I didn't feel good about myself . . . It's strange hitting someone in the face when you've got nothing against them.'

After the match the boxers, who had never met before, went for a pint together. Ricky said he would keep up some exercise but admitted it was 'back to cheese sarnies'.

For someone as upfront in his distaste for showbiz 'charidee' types, Ricky lent his name to a number of worthy causes – sometimes without thought for his personal comfort, as the boxing bout had shown. Such was his profile after the first series of *The Office* that Comic Relief were quick to pop the question: would he participate in Red Nose Day? He would – in a sketch alongside boy band Blue, to whom he attempted to teach some dubious dance moves, prior to their performance on *Top of the Pops*.

But his appearance was also a masterclass in self-deprecation. On his journey to meet the boys (supposedly by chauffeur-driven limousine), as the car sped through scenes of urban decay and deprivation, Ricky would often look up, take in the grim landscape, and assume a pose of concern before immersing himself in the *Radio Times*. Closer inspection of the cover revealed its reader described as 'The Most Influential Man In British Comedy'.

He wasn't yet, but he was well on the way. And he knew it.

8

—

Farewell Wernham Hogg

❝ *My dad used to hod-carry, but I think that doing six TV shows, being driven around in a Mercedes, is hard work. For God's sake, I'm an artist!* ❞

DAVID BRENT had become one of the major comic figures in British TV history, rivalling the impact John Cleese made with Basil Fawlty in the 1970s. The character had captured the nation's imagination in a big way, easily eclipsing recent favourites such as Steve Coogan's TV presenter Alan Partridge and Richard Wilson's grumpy old man Victor Meldrew in *One Foot in the Grave*. The supposed 'faux fly-on-the-wall documentary that introduced viewers to the delusional, isolated world of office manager David Brent' had taken on a life of its own.

So it was a huge surprise when Gervais and Merchant announced that enough was enough and that after two forty-minute Christmas specials broadcast on 26 and 27 December 2003, they wouldn't write any further episodes of *The Office*. 'I think that will be the end of it,' said actor Martin Freeman to BBC America. Though new acting projects would soon be in the offing, he and his fellow *Office* actors must have been disappointed to see the gravy train hit the buffers.

Although the end of an era was beckoning, the Christmas specials were full of treats for viewers to get their post-turkey teeth into. The first began with Brent in even worse shape than he had been at the end of series two. Despite his unhappiness with the way that he had been presented in the documentary series made about Wernham Hogg, it had nevertheless turned him into a Z-list celebrity, and, while he was a travelling salesman by day, he was also being paid to make personal appearances at various different nightclubs in the evenings. There was even a pop promo video for his self-funded single.

But underneath the superficial fare he desperately missed the camaraderie provided by office life, and still paid visits to see his former colleagues at the paper merchants where Gareth now had his job. All in all he had become a sad figure of a man. Meanwhile, when he wasn't playing tricks on Gareth, Tim pined for Dawn, who was still in Florida with Lee.

However, there appeared to be a glimmer of hope for all concerned when the production company decided to make a follow-up programme about the Wernham Hogg Christmas party, even offering to fly Dawn and Lee home for the event. To add to Brent's discomfort and sense of impotence, former boss Neil and old mucker Finchy asked him to bring a date along to the party, while an appearance as part of a *Blind Date*-style stunt at a nightclub went horrifically wrong.

Even though the specials went out on BBC1 (not on BBC2, as the two series had) as highlights of its seasonal schedule, Gervais and Merchant were insistent that the formula wasn't going to be watered down in any way for mass consumption, and the shows were deliberately kept 'dark and slow burning'. There was still no laughter track, no promise of a traditional happy ending – and indeed the Corporation's bosses didn't even know the running times until the programmes were in post-production.

The second part of the special opened with Brent indulging in some Internet dating to find someone to take to the party – in typical fashion, both dates he went on were disastrous. Then, after a particularly awful nightclub gig, he informed his agent that he was sick and tired of doing them. When he visited the office with his dog, Neil told him that he could no longer just turn up unannounced. Only Tim's offer to go for a drink with him saved his former boss from one final, gutting humiliation.

Meanwhile, Tim and Dawn were reunited in their old environment and, once again, Dawn mentioned her hopes of becoming an illustrator – an ambition boyfriend Lee later rubbished at the party. A depressed Brent turned up at the bash to find that his date Carol was both nice-looking and interested in him. Buoyed by her desire to see him again, he finally summoned up the courage to tell both Neil and Finchy to 'f**k off'.

Trudy's 'secret Santa' scheme for staff to buy each other presents played an unexpected part in getting Tim and Dawn's romance back on the rails: having got in the taxi with Lee, Dawn unwrapped her present to discover a paintbox from Tim with a note saying, 'Never give up.'

She returned to the party to reconnect with Tim, Brent and Gareth, and the series went out on a wave of hope that the star-crossed lovers might finally make a go of it and that personally, if not career-wise, Brent might finally have made good.

As to be expected, there was a huge build-up for the specials in the media, and this was reflected in viewing figures. The first show attracted an audience of 7.2 million – and, though the second dropped by just over a million, perhaps because those unfamiliar with the show found its tone and low-key approach unappealing on first viewing, this was still impressive in the most congested broadcasting season of the year. Furthermore, the following year would also see the two-part Christmas special rewarded with two BAFTA wins in April (one for Ricky for Best Comedy Performance, and the other for Best Sitcom), and two nominations at the British Comedy Awards in December.

In retrospect, *The Office* was hardly Christmas fare in the tradition of comedy favourites Morecambe and Wise or *Only Fools and Horses*, nor was it fast-food humour like *Little Britain*. Therefore, it was only likely to tap into its original audience or latecomers who had picked up on it via the repeats. Commercially, there may have been a demand for a third series but, Gervais noted, 'We thought we might have blown it by doing the Christmas specials. We could have packed it a little bit tighter and probably put it all in two series.'

The writers felt that they'd gone as far as they could with it without having to repeat themselves, and the specials seem to have confirmed this. So the old team of Brent, Gareth, Tim and Dawn posing for a final shot for the TV crew was the last the public was to see of *The Office*. The programme that had so painfully yet so accurately captured the atmosphere of contemporary working life had closed its doors for the last time.

Meanwhile, plans were already being hatched to produce an American counterpart. BBC America had broadcast the original first series in January 2003, and the reaction had been generally positive. The *LA Times* attempted to clue in its readers thus: 'Imagine a television series about mid-level workers stuck in dead-end jobs. Now imagine producing it without big stars, laugh tracks, tidy endings or glamour.'

Critics felt that some of its subtleties had been lost on the majority of US viewers, but, remembering that Gervais and Merchant were big fans of popular US TV series like *Seinfeld* and *The Larry Sanders Show*, one can understand how it might appeal to a more high-brow American mentality.

BBC America was a digital channel available only to a small percentage of US viewers, and this meant the average size of an audience for *The Office* was around 350,000. But, as was the case with Ricky's phenomenal rise to fame in Britain, luck was once again on *The Office*'s side. One year later, on 25 January 2004, this British export unexpectedly won two Golden Globes – an award given by the Hollywood Foreign Press Association. Trouncing previous heavyweight winners *Will and Grace* and *Sex and the City*, it won in the Best Comedy category. And Gervais won Best Comedy Actor, which was no mean achievement when he was up against the likes of Matt LeBlanc from *Friends* and Eric McCormack from *Will and Grace*.

What was even more remarkable was that *The Office* was the first British show to be nominated – indeed it only gained admission because BBC America partly funded the production of its second series. Gervais, Merchant, producer Ash Atalla and actors Lucy Davis and Martin Freeman dutifully turned up at the awards ceremony, but felt they had little chance of winning anything. In fact, the cameras were not even trained on the unknown Brits' table, which was probably just as well, as Ricky quipped that his group looked 'like something you'd pay a shilling to see in a tent a hundred years ago'!

On returning home from the Golden Globe awards ceremony in Los Angeles with the two statuettes, his memories were typically more precious than the awards themselves: 'Here I am, this fat bloke from Reading, sharing a room with Jack Nicholson. It's absolutely fantastic.'

An unlikely spin-off predicted from the US success of the series was an influx of American sightseers to Slough. Even though, as Gervais himself giggled, 'There are some people in Britain who haven't heard of it,' Slough's mayor, Councillor Laurie Gleeson, was rubbing his hands in anticipation. 'Hopefully, it will put us on the map and, rather than tourists going to the Tower of London or Stratford-upon-Avon, they might like to visit Slough.'

It was, to be fair, a slim hope. But there again, who would have predicted the rise of a young man from the drab, grey Reading council estate of Whitley to the top of the entertainment tree? As for the people of his hometown, he admitted to the *Mirror* in 2001: 'I don't think [they] are very happy that I've put them on the map. They're probably thinking, "Why can't a proper celebrity like that lovely Davina McCall or Graham Norton have come from Reading instead of that fat bloke? He's *rubbish!*"'

With regard to adapting the sitcom to a US setting, plans had already been laid and the awards no doubt speeded up this process. An American version of *The Office* had first been mooted in August 2003, and Greg Daniels, a regular writer for *The Simpsons* and co-creator of *King of the Hill,* was brought on board to develop the idea further. Within a week of the Golden Globes, NBC TV announced that a pilot would go into pre-production and the cast was revealed. Provisionally entitled *The Office: An American Workplace,* the show starred Steve Carell as Michael Scott, the boss from hell.

Carell was already known to viewers for his work on programmes like *Saturday Night Live* and through a couple of well-timed roles in recent movies. For example, he'd almost stolen the show from Jim Carrey with his part as the obnoxious television newscaster in *Bruce Almighty,* and had received excellent reviews for his part as cerebrally challenged weather forecaster Brick Tamland in *The Anchorman.*

The US adaptation was initially surprisingly faithful to its Brit parent: done in the same mockumentary style, it followed the daily interactions of a group of eccentric workers at the Dunder Mifflin paper supply company in Scranton, Pennsylvania. Some of the characters closely resembled those of the British series – there was mildly righteous receptionist Pam Beesly, played by Jenna Fischer, bored but talented salesman Jim Halpert (John Krasinski) and his obsequious, almost sociopathic, nemesis and volunteer sheriff, Dwight Schrute (Rainn Wilson).

While David Brent was flawed but ultimately benign, Carell played his new role with a different kind of energy. Michael Scott believed himself to be the perfect boss, but he was a much more psychopathic character – he was smooth and well dressed with perfect hair, the kind of man who got to the top by being belittling, intimidating and aggressive. A man with a true appetite for power. Yet there were also similarities. Just as David Brent was fond of quoting the Two Ronnies, Michael Scott constantly referred to his love of the Three Stooges.

The overall tone was similar, with mundane settings and no laughter track, and the result was, against the odds, a finely observed parody of US water-cooler culture. There was, of course, more emphasis placed on issues relevant only to the American workplace, such as employees having to cope with Scott's mishandled downgrading of their health insurance. The racist remarks – usually a no-no on US prime-time TV – were also fine-tuned to the American sensibility, but were present nonetheless.

The pilot was based heavily on the BBC's original episode and suffered a little from trying to shoehorn its new American characters into the British script. However, by the third episode, just as its audience started to tail off, it began to hit its stride, and, in spite of average reviews when it was first aired in March 2005 – *Time* magazine alone noting its 'daring, unflinching take on very American workplace tensions' – *The Office*'s US sibling would eventually win through.

Ricky was adamant that the scriptwriters had done a

superb job of adapting his original concept to make it appeal to an American audience: 'It is as good,' he insisted to *Entertainment Weekly*. 'I love the fact that, apart from the first one, the scripts are all original. You've gone back to the blueprint of what the characters are and you've started from there, as opposed to copying anything . . . To me it was like watching something I had nothing to do with, and it would be my new favourite sitcom. I purposefully had no involvement. It should be made for Americans by Americans.'

Far from being over-protective about his baby, Gervais seemed more concerned that the show wouldn't reach its potential viewing public and get dropped by the channel. 'The danger is that, on NBC, it won't get the viewers they need, but [they deserve] rounds of applause for being true to it. They're good, but the stakes are so much higher. If it doesn't get a ten per cent on the first night, they'll panic. The reason the rumour that it was cancelled went round is that it got the lowest ever score on the NBC focus group. That's a coincidence. It got the lowest ever on BBC2 as well.'

He needn't have worried. The success of the US series was due in no small part to the fact that NBC believed in the show from the off and backed it to the hilt. It was possibly motivated in this by the demise of two of its flagship sitcoms, *Friends* and *Frasier*, in 2004, and the need to find a successful replacement, so a further five episodes were commissioned. The show eventually went into its third season with average viewing figures of over ten million per week.

The network had bravely refused to cancel it in the face of a diminishing audience during its first run, mindful of the history of *Seinfeld* – another sleeper that eventually hit pay dirt for the channel. Their faith would be amply rewarded, with Steve Carell going on to win a Golden Globe for Best Performance by an Actor in a Television Series (Musical or Comedy) in 2006, the same award Ricky had won two years previously for the original British series.

Its team of writers was also nominated for three Writers Guild of America awards in 2005 – Best Comedy Series, Best New Series, and Best Episodic Comedy – and in 2006 for three more, from the Television Critics Association, two of which it won – Outstanding Achievement in Comedy, and Individual Achievement in Comedy (Steve Carell).

Talking about the success of the US series, an elated Gervais (who was credited as its executive producer) remarked, 'This is great news. The American version is now getting all the acclaim of the original – and it deserves it. Steve Carell is amazing, as is the entire cast and writing team.' And in a case of coals to Newcastle, the US version of *The Office* received its first UK airing on BBC3 on 14 June 2005.

Such was the original's universal appeal that Gervais and Merchant's brainchild was eventually acquired by pay-channel Canal Plus and adapted for a French audience as *Le Bureau*. Set in a grim office block in a riot-torn Paris suburb, David Brent had mutated into fifty-something Gilles Triquet, '*le boss trop cool*', of the Cogirep paper company, prone to quips like, 'Zat's life!' More of a monster than his Berkshire counterpart, Triquet was a bigoted, chauvinistic man played by well-known French TV actor François Berléand.

Pranks involving pungent cheese may have replaced jokes about jelly, but many of the prototype's characters were there, including a military-obsessed jobsworth who made models of the Battle of Austerlitz. First screened in May 2006, the show was seen by many as a perfect portrait of modern France, and French newspaper *Le Figaro* hailed it as 'dark and hilarious'.

In Britain, the series had become a mega success, with David Brent soundalike bores in every school, pub, building site and army hut across the land – but how was its creator going to come up with something equally successful? *The Office* had effortlessly entered the public's collective consciousness. Could Gervais produce another winner?

In the short term, the answer was a sidestep into live work, and, unlike most of his peers on the comedy circuit, it was something of which he had had little experience. Taking an overview of Ricky's roundabout rise to the top, only a few of the traditional stepping stones to success are in evidence, but fame has given him the chance to fill in some of the gaps, the most notable being performing live in front of an audience with no opportunity for retakes. Since the heady days of the Comedy Store in the 1980s, many comedians have used stand-up as a stepladder to screen success, and it would have been easy to assume that Ricky Gervais was one of that number, but this is not the case.

He managed to bypass that toughest of learning curves, yet has remained fascinated by the genre. It's possible he still has a residual envy at writing partner Stephen Merchant's early sallies into stand-up, but what Ricky appears to treasure is the fact that each night is different. Having engineered his classic comedy creations to take up just so much time and no more, carefully measuring the laughs per minute and ensuring a satisfying conclusion for both him and the viewers, flying by the seat of his pants and displaying his impromptu wit has proved to possess an understandable attraction.

Television, of course, lacks that primal emotional connection with the audience, the gladiatorial thumbs up or down that can seal a performer's fate in a matter of minutes. Fortunately for him, though, it's unlikely that Ricky will feel the hot breath of a disapproving audience on the back of his neck any time soon, and he readily confesses that guilt lies at the heart of his stand-up urge. 'Most comedians slog around the country for fifteen years playing to students in grotty venues in the vague hope that someone will give them their own TV show,' he has said to the press. 'I waltzed in and wrote a sitcom, and now I feel I should have done the bits I missed.'

Thus, in January 2003, he found himself playing a limited two-week season in the intimate and very local surroundings of the Bloomsbury Theatre. A self-confessed fan of nature programmes since his biology-student days, Ricky turned his gaze on wildlife and presented a one-man show, *Animals,* subtitled 'Life on Earth (the bits David Attenborough left out)'.

He'd test-driven the material the previous July at the Soho Theatre with a show described as reflecting a 'fascination with the animal kingdom. I'll start off with the Bible and how the snake stitched everything up for God right from the beginning.' On the subject of beginnings, the comic would enter (and later exit) the stage to the refrain of Suede's hit single 'Animal Nitrate' – one of several in-jokes for the cognoscenti to savour.

His biggest worry about the hour-long show was that he had never before 'had to go that long without sitting down or eating'. *The Times*'s Clive Davis had nevertheless been impressed, stating that, 'While this show may have its flaws, it also boasts moments of unmistakeable genius. For someone who does not consider himself to be a stand-up performer, Gervais turns in a compellingly confident display.'

The Soho Theatre stint had sold out immediately, and only a lucky few thousand witnessed the comic live on stage on this occasion too. Tickets for the Bloomsbury were selling on the black market for £150, well in excess of their face value – which was a pity as Ricky had attempted to make the show affordable to all.

'I don't think I can begin to justify people paying something like £25 to see me,' he told London listings magazine *Time Out*. 'That's not false modesty, it's because I want to give value for money. Sixty dates in thousand-seaters – I think that's cabaret. That's clowning. That's shouting. I don't jump and shout. I want people to see the face. With my stand-up it should be more like watching TV.'

For somebody who saw himself as neither a stand-up comedian nor an actor, this first foray on to the boards was a triumph. He may still have had to earn his spurs to become a fully fledged Eddie Izzard, but by common consent Gervais delivered the goods. Of course, he had an audience of *Office* aficionados to cheer him on. Talking about the material for his latest venture, which came together in a couple of days while filming *The*

Office, Ricky commented, 'It's anecdotes and stories, not high-intensity gag-writing. That's why it was easy to cobble together.'

The scattershot approach allowed for plenty of digressions, leaping from sex to childhood to war . . . and back to more sex. There was an inspired film clip which preceded Ricky on to the stage – a sequence of fornicating lions with the comedian's voice-over carefully pitched somewhere between a BBC nature series and a sleazy European soft-porn movie. He poked fun at targets as disparate as King Kong and wheelchair-bound scientist Stephen Hawking, and had fun with a series of slides depicting homosexual animals. He delivered a deadpan list of little-known facts about the animal kingdom and there was a brilliant dissection of the biblical Genesis story.

Although fans lapped it up, the media was less impressed. While *The Observer* raved, 'Gervais has proved that he is a remarkably talented performer on stage as well as on screen,' *The Daily Telegraph* noted that, 'When he comes back on for a brief sob story about his childhood, flashing a glimpse of the real Ricky, you realize how little substance there's been to sink one's teeth into.'

Even Clive Davis of *The Times,* who had lauded the previous year's trial run, felt the script sagged 'whenever he plays for some rather easy bad-taste laughs. Even if the audience was willing to indulge some of the ropier moments, it was mildly depressing to hear him scrabble around for chuckles on the subject of Anne Frank and the kind of bike-shed banter prized by every fourteen-year-old boy in the land. This would barely pass muster on a quiet night at a comedy club, and it sounds no more clever here, even given a post-modern gloss.'

Perhaps it was reassuring that not everyone appreciated all that Ricky Gervais did. And, one suspected, that was exactly the way he liked it.

9

Animals and Flanimals

*If you're thinking you'll be getting Monty Python,
you're gonna be upset. It's on two levels but . . .*
Flanimals *is meant to make eight-year-olds giggle.*

As *The Office* continued its global progress to becoming
the BBC's most successful comedy export of all time,
being aired in some eighty countries and scooping its
creators yet more awards, Ricky busied himself with a
number of other projects, no doubt contemplating all
the while his next big comedy success.

Early in 2004, he made a cameo non-comedy appearance as an Irish terrorist in season three of fast-paced
American TV thriller series *Alias*, which starred Jennifer
Garner as Sydney Bristow. The episode, 'Façade', saw him
join a star-studded tradition of special guests that already
included David Cronenberg, Quentin Tarantino, Ethan
Hawke and Roger Moore. He was a bomb-making boffin
with a vendetta against the person who killed his brother

– who just happened to be Sydney Bristow. 'It was a bigger part than I first thought,' he quipped on *Friday Night with Jonathan Ross*. 'Me being serious . . . I can't watch it.'

He had thought he'd made a decent fist of the challenge of playing it straight 'until one evening I switched on [satellite channel] UK Gold and saw Mel Smith being completely unconvincing in a serious part in *Minder*. I thought, "Jesus Christ, that's me in *Alias!*" I'm worried people might think this part is vanity. But I hope they'll be reassured when they see it. Everyone else is in Armani suits and I'm in a chunky-knit sweater and Hush Puppies. I look like Gyles Brandreth at a *Vogue* fashion shoot. So I've managed to retain my credibility as someone completely unglamorous – nothing can interrupt that. I still look stupid.'

In the spring, encouraged by the success of *Animals* and its DVD release, he undertook his first national tour. This time he presented a one-man show entitled *Politics*. Talking about it, to *The Observer*, he commented, 'I know what I want to see. I want to see me acting like Seinfeld.'

Ricky came to the tour on a high, and wasn't shy of letting people know his mood. 'Obviously, I decided to do these gigs (some in the north) before I won the Golden Globes and I'm told, annoyingly, that I am legally obliged to at least turn up. Luckily, the plane journey back from Los Angeles is ten hours, so there was plenty of time to write a brand new show and watch *The Lord of the Rings* trilogy.' He explained to his audience that he would be doing his 'usual brand of brilliant, irreverent yet observational comedy', which would cover subjects as diverse as 'meeting Jack Nicholson, driving

Soulmates: After meeting at the university bar in 1982, Ricky and partner Jane Fallon have remained together ever since, but have not married.

The first of many: In April 2002, BAFTA awards were presented to Ricky for Best Comedy Performance, and to the whole team for Best Situation Comedy (*from left to right:* Anil Gupta, Ash Atalla, Stephen Merchant and Ricky Gervais).

Success beckons in the USA: After a positive response to airings of the series on BBC America, in January 2004 *The Office* won a Golden Globe for Best Television Series (Musical or Comedy), while Ricky also received the coveted award for his unique portrayal of David Brent.

The best of friends: TV and radio presenter Jonathan Ross (*above right, at a charity quiz night*) has become firm friends with Ricky over the last few years. In each of Ricky's appearances on *Friday Night with Jonathan Ross*, a hilarious battle of wits has ensued.

A valiant effort: In 2005 Ricky joined Ewan McGregor (*right*) in the cast of animated film *Valiant*, in which he voiced the character of Bugsy, 'a streetwise, independent con man of a pigeon'.

The much anticipated follow-up to *The Office* came in the form of *Extras*, which was first broadcast in July 2005. Following the fortunes of two struggling bit-part actors played by Ricky and Ashley Jensen (*left*), the series also featured a fine performance by Stephen Merchant (*above right*) as Ricky's useless agent.

Each episode featured at least one well-known celebrity, all of whom had been keen to get involved in the project, including notable A-listers such as Kate Winslet (*above*) and Patrick Stewart (*below*), as well as US actors Ben Stiller and Samuel L. Jackson.

Despite his many work commitments, Ricky still makes time for charity events. On 2 July 2005 he appeared at the Live 8 benefit concert in Hyde Park, London, and to the delight of the crowd did a rare repeat performance of his famous *Office* monkey dance. Eight months later, at the Royal Albert Hall, Ricky took part in a benefit show for the Teenage Cancer Trust alongside a host of stand-up acts including Robin Ince (*right*).

In December 2005, Ricky took the opportunity to conduct an on-screen interview with one of his comedy heroes, US actor, writer, producer, film director, and star of *Curb Your Enthusiasm*, Larry David. The two appeared to establish a good rapport, both mutually respectful of the other's achievements in the entertainment world.

It was a dream come true when Matt Groening, creator of *The Simpsons* and self-confessed fan of *The Office*, asked Ricky to write and appear in an episode of the award-winning cartoon series, which was broadcast in spring 2006. Groening noted admiringly of his collaboration with Ricky, 'Everything you could possibly want from Ricky Gervais you get.'

Success around every corner: In May 2006, it was revealed that the series of podcasts Ricky had produced with Stephen Merchant and Karl Pilkington (*above left*) had been downloaded by so many listeners that it would officially become known as 'the world's most successful podcast' in the 2007 edition of *Guinness World Records.*

The sky's the limit: Since enjoying his first commercial success with *The Office*, Ricky Gervais appears destined to succeed in every project upon which he embarks, which begs the question – where does he go from here?

around in limos and not putting my hand in my pocket once'.

Taking in dates in Newcastle, Birmingham, York, Oxford, Glasgow and Manchester in April, Ricky concluded with week-long engagements at the Bloomsbury Theatre, followed by the Palace Theatre in London in late May. Posters for the show featured the comic adopting the legendary pose of Cuba's famous freedom fighter Che Guevara, though there was also a look of 1970s sit-com revolutionary Citizen Smith about him as well.

Able support came from friend and fellow comic Robin Ince, with whom he'd last shared a stage during the *Rubbernecker* show in Edinburgh. Ince had first met Gervais back in 1992 when the latter – in Robin's words, 'now the nation's funniest man and leading Reg Varney lookalike' – was still an ents manager. They later worked together on *The 11 O'Clock Show* and *Meet Ricky Gervais*, while Ince's other work as a writer included sketches for such hit TV series as the *Live Floor Show, V Graham Norton* and *Have I Got News For You.*

The tour saw the pair fill 2,000-seat venues like Manchester Opera House, despite an almost total lack of publicity. In Robin Ince's words, 'There were no . . . flyers or newspaper ads, just the rumours that the man with the Golden Globes who did that funny dance is coming to your town.'

The show was only loosely based on politics, and took in numerous targets such as cerebral palsy charity SCOPE to the Holocaust and paedophilia. Ricky's onstage character had something of the oafish bigot about him, a feature strongly reminiscent of his *11 O'Clock Show* character. His hour-long set began with a short film featuring him standing outside the Houses of Parliament observing, 'You don't have to come here to see politics – politics is everywhere,' before tipping a 'little fella' out of his wheelchair – inevitably, in reality, long-suffering *Office* producer Ash Atalla.

The live section ran the gamut of everything from Stephen Hawking – 'the most intelligent man on the planet and I'm having a go' – to nursery rhymes such as Jack and Jill and Humpty Dumpty ('don't send horses to perform medical services – they haven't got the dexterity – they can't even scrub up') to the late Conservative MP Stephen Milligan, who was found dead wearing a pair of ladies' tights and a plastic bag over his head, after an auto-erotic practice had gone wrong.

Gervais also drew on his days at college to talk about leaflets. Indeed, the funniest moment of the show was when he ran down a ten-point plan from a leaflet apparently issued by the Terrence Higgins Trust about Aids entitled 'You know you don't always have to have anal sex.' Explaining the content of the literature, which revealed an array of eye-opening yet creative ways that gay men could have fun with a partner without resorting to anal sex, Ricky clearly enjoyed sharing the bizarreness of the information as much as the audience enjoyed hearing it.

Talking about the subject matter of his latest project, Ricky commented, 'It's not serious. I write the jokes so they go the wrong way. Like "Nelson Mandela: incarcerated for twenty-five years. Out fourteen and hasn't reoffended, which goes to show that prison works." My targets are weak ones . . . not dictatorships.'

When the show was eventually released on DVD, one of the bonus features was a documentary of life on the road with Ricky and Robin Ince, shot during the actual tour. Entitled *Living With Ricky*, it revealed a telling side to the comedian's character via his supposed infatuation with fellow funnyman Ince. Shot on a hand-held camera, it featured Ricky regularly concealing himself and suddenly springing out in front of his travelling partner. Gervais quipped, 'One of the reasons I did this tour was so I got him [Ince] away from home; he was all mine.' Talking about Ricky's numerous pranks, Robin offered, 'People will think fame has gone to his head, but it's quietened him down.'

Ricky was shown regularly communicating with Ince in a series of shouts and non-verbal mumbo jumbo, about which Robin said, 'It was like being with someone who's got a mental illness, a dementia.' At one point, Ince astutely compared Gervais to the late comic genius Spike Milligan, deciding that 'the British public loved Ricky because they didn't have to work with him.'

In a pre-tour interview, Ince likened Ricky to 'an eighteenth-century European child emperor veering between bouncing noisy glee as he knocks the hats off his courtiers and then sudden dreadful wrath when his meat-on-a-stick and nut selection is late'.

So had success spoilt Ricky Gervais? 'No,' said Ince. 'He was always this way. It's just now that his screaming and gurning in a high street can be stopped by someone shouting out: "Oi mate, do the dance!" After that, I know I'll get a couple of minutes of embarrassed peace . . .'

Fortunately for Ince, he was soon to be freed from the ceaseless torments of his friend and nemesis when Ricky embarked on another solo project, namely the writing of his first book. *Flanimals,* which was published in October 2004, was a labour of love about a bunch of surreal, ugly creatures with weird and wonderful names who lead dark, brutal existences. Intended for children, it had started out as a simple way of entertaining a young member of the family and had taken on a life of its own. How much it owed to his biology studies must be left to the imagination . . .

Asked in a *Sun* webchat about the inspiration behind *Flanimals,* Ricky said, 'I used to do it to make my nephew laugh, and I used to draw these little creatures from when I was a teenager. He grew out of it and I continued thinking it was hilarious until the age of forty-four. It's just real fun. I do it for the same reason that I act – I enjoy it. Acting's fun and so is coming up with ridiculous creatures. I like the wordplay and sketching them out. I like to see how stupid and weird I can get.'

Ricky asked a long-time friend, artist Rob Steen, to draw a couple of the creatures from his initial sketches. 'I thought they looked great. Mine had been little pencil drawings and I thought that it'd be funny to impose this on the world. We did a couple of mock-ups and it was one of those things that was always on the back-burner. Then obviously, with my new-found success, publishers were more receptive to the idea and it got published. It did really well and was a number one title. Hopefully that's because the book was fun and not because they were buying it as it was from "the bloke who did *The Office*".'

Prefaced by a simple introduction, the book consists of three chapters. The first section, The Spotter's Guide, takes the young reader into an Edward Lear-like universe populated by fifty-six different creatures with names like Clunge Ambler, Frappled Humpdumbler and Dweezle Muzzgrub.

These were bound to catch the imagination of kids who, as Gervais pointed out, 'like gruesome stuff. They like gore.' They were inventions that sat comfortably in the realms of children's fiction next to the likes of Raymond Briggs's *Fungus the Bogeyman*. Ricky lovingly described his new creations to anyone who asked. In a *Sunday Times* interview, for example, the Clunge Ambler is revealed to be 'a sweaty little waddle-gimp'. This poor little creature likes to shuffle around trying to cuddle things, but because it is 'weird and smells' it is forever being beaten up and then buried. Rather like an abused dog that still returns to its sadistic master, the Clunge Ambler then goes in search of the Flanimal that buried him to give it a cuddle, only to end up being buried again. The Wobboid Mump, on the other hand, is essentially an eye encased in jelly, whose time is spent looking for a reason for its existence. It is destined never to find a reason, however, because the Wobboid Mump is blind.

Once introduced, these bizarre and faintly disgusting characters are further developed in the Flanimal Behaviour section, after which readers are quizzed on just how much knowledge they have now acquired about the Flanimal universe. Here and there snatches of pure Gervais humour can be discerned. 'Loads of Flanimals were hurt during the making of this book,' is the proud boast printed on the dust jacket's flap.

The book has gone on to sell almost a quarter of a million copies in the UK, and a further volume, *More*

Flanimals, appeared a year later. It was as instant a hit as its predecessor, with the US edition leaping straight into the *New York Times* bestseller list at number eight.

In creative terms, this was not a cash-in but an improvement on the debut which, in truth, had relied as much on Rob Steen's superb and grotesque illustrations as it had on Gervais's descriptions, written in a style similar to that of the late British comedian and wordsmith Stanley Unwin. Now, with the introduction of new favourites like Plappavom and Skwunt, Gervais actually concocted a proper narrative, such as a passage about a baby Blunging, which suggested his creations might enjoy some longevity.

Indeed, this was a much-desired ambition. 'I didn't want this to be Ricky Gervais's *Flanimals*,' he explained to the *Sun Online* as the second volume appeared, and spoke about a planned film adaptation of his cartoon characters. 'We're hopefully going to try to do a little short movie first, then work on the main film, because it takes so long . . . I want it to last longer than me. I want it to be up there with the *Mr Men* books and *Doctor Seuss*, so this film is fantastic to be working on. I'm really getting into things being created on the page; there's no ad-libbing. If a leaf falls from a tree in a cartoon, that was painstakingly drawn and I like the freedom and the total control you have over that.

'It's going to be an $80-million-dollar movie, which will take three years to make so it's a big deal. I've got my wish list for voices. I want to get Danny DeVito . . . Samuel Jackson would be amazing, too. I haven't even worked out how all of them sound. Some don't make any noises, which is going to be fun! If you write an opera or a play it's a creative process. If it's a cartoon it's called making stuff up!'

Given his punishing schedule, it was remarkable that Gervais could find time to go out and promote his publication, signing copies at Borders bookshop in London's West End and satisfying hordes of fans in a queue that snaked out of the door and went along Oxford Street for several hundred yards.

Amidst the mad whirl of publicity, while Ricky was preoccupied with amassing awards and writing new material for numerous different projects, a more serious matter was to be resolved in March 2005 when the case of a group of fraudsters came to court. Two years previously, the gang had stolen his identity and tried to take money from his account, but fortunately their efforts to swindle him were ultimately foiled. Although this type of offence is said to be one of the fastest-rising crimes of the new millennium, it surely took a different class of criminal idiot to attempt to become Ricky Gervais, one of the most easily recognizable faces of the millennium.

In a bizarre incident that Gervais would have binned as 'too unlikely' had it emerged from his own imagination, the fraudsters succeeded in taking a cool £200,000 from his bank account. In a move that was either supremely audacious or, more likely, stupid, the criminals had cut out a picture of the comic from *The Office* DVD and pasted it on to a dead man's passport.

Then, using an insider in the bank, they had managed to transfer funds from his account. Only when they had tried to use the money to buy bullion had they been rumbled and apprehended by the police.

At their trial, the fraudsters each went to prison for between two and two and a half years. Prosecutor John Dodd named bullion dealer Anthony Baird as the man who spotted the scam. 'Mr Baird was something of a fan of Mr Gervais. It would seem that some of those involved in the attempted fraud were not. As a result of Mr Baird's suspicions, police were alerted . . .'

Ricky recounted his version of the whole bizarre story to *Q* magazine a few months later. 'What happened was, some people pretended to be me, to buy gold. What they did was, they stole a passport and changed the picture. The picture they put in was me on the front cover of *The Office*. So it's David Brent like that [Brent pose]. And funnily enough they got caught! That would be great, wouldn't it? The bank goes, "Are you really Ricky Gervais?" and they go [does The Dance, with sound effects] and they give them the gold and they get away.'

Later that same month, events would take a turn for the better, when Gervais's long-held love of animation came to the fore and, for the first time, he supplied the voice of a movie cartoon character. He did, however, have a little previous TV form. 'I did a couple of lines for Comic Relief in *Robbie the Reindeer* about four years ago. I was a penguin . . . Why do I keep doing fat birds?'

Valiant, a Disney creation tagged 'from the producer of *Shrek* and *Shrek 2*', told the story of a lowly wood pigeon who overcame his diminutive size to become a hero in the Royal Air Force's Homing Pigeon Service during the Second World War. The RHPS (which did actually exist) advanced the Allied cause by flying vital messages about enemy movements across the English Channel, while evading brutal attacks by the enemy's Falcon Brigade.

Though it swiftly migrated to video for the 2005 Christmas DVD market, Ricky 'liked the story'. He was less convinced, however, by his own performance. 'I think I was rubbish for the first day, I didn't know what I was doing, because it's so alien to me. There are no other actors there and so you're acting blind, so to speak.'

He played Bugsy, described in the film's publicity as 'a street-wise, independent con man of a pigeon'. 'They wanted my character to be big and over the top, and be a real Cockney wide boy,' Ricky told the BBC website. 'And I was just thinking, "I can't do that, that's not what I do. I do naturalistic acting! I remember saying to them after about an hour, "I think you should have got Bob Hoskins." And all the producers sort of looked at each other and went, "He's right."

'But then they let me ad-lib a little bit more and do my own thing, and I sort of crossed it between my stand-up persona – which is a brasher, cockier version of myself, but still very vulnerable – and Bob Hope and Woody Allen, because he's a reluctant hero and a bit of a coward. By the end I kept wanting to start again and I'd keep saying, "*Now* I know what you want!" So the director must have been very patient and probably kept on thinking, "Why *didn't* we get Bob Hoskins?"'

Ricky revealed that Ewan McGregor (who played the eponymous hero) had been a big help to him after they encountered each other for the first time in the smallest room. 'I went into the toilet and was having a wee. He came in and went, "You all right?" I said, "Yeah, I just don't think I'm any good at this. It's the shouting, I just can't do it." And he said, "Aye, I know what you mean. You don't want to feel like you're a ****, do you?" I thought, "Yeah, he's right, I really shouldn't worry about it". And after that I went out and it was great. See, to people like Ewan it's second nature. But for me, I had trouble just reading the script, that's why I was making it up as I went along.'

Director Gary Chapman was pleased with the results, telling the press, 'It was a new challenge for Ricky. He was used to writing and performing his own material, but once he got his character, he let loose and added something special. You'd throw something at him, and he would just go with it. He has this comedic spontaneity that stand-up comedy breeds.'

'It was a pleasure to be part of *Valiant*,' Gervais concluded, adding: 'I have always wanted to be a big mouthy bird!'

10

Anyone for Extras?

*⁶ In real life, the funniest people are the people you know.
If you can create this familiarity and invest it in your
characters . . . everything feels real. ⁹*

EVENTUALLY, after a period of time working apart
from his friend and co-writer Stephen Merchant, the
time had come to face the challenge of producing a
follow-up to their mega hit. It was a project he
approached, on the surface at least, with a winning
mixture of confidence and level-headedness. 'It's not a
competition,' he told *The Observer*, 'and if I lose against
The Office, I've still won because I did *The Office*. Did I beat
my own record? No. Who cares? How do you beat *The
Office*? Ratings? Means nothing. Being around for longer?
This will be two series, too. Awards? How do you beat six
Baftas and two Golden Globes? That's mental. That
record's safe. But did I have good fun making it? Yeah.
Could I have had more fun in the past two years? No . . .'

Fame and fortune had apparently not turned the funny man's head. 'Ego is a dangerous thing,' he later elaborated. 'The day you wake up and think, "Of course I could make a film like *The Matrix*," is also the day you hope a voice somewhere will still be saying, "Aw, Rick, settle down – what you are good at is very small-scale comedy, stick to that."'

The ever shrewd and pragmatic Gervais had never intended to create a conventional follow-up to *The Office*. But in creating *Extras*, a six-episode sitcom about bit-part actors working on movies, with Stephen, he was able to exploit his success and include well-known names in his cast – the polar opposite to *The Office*'s 'everyday people'. Yet in some ways his new venture into small-screen comedy was just as off the wall as his first hit had been.

Ricky was to star as leading character Andy Millman, a former bank worker who had left his full-time job several years previously in order to follow his dream of becoming an actor. Unfortunately, success in the acting world had so far managed to elude him, and without any decent speaking roles coming his way, he'd had to rely on 'extra' work to get by.

Millman was more intelligent than David Brent, with more of a chip on his shoulder and certainly a bit more self-aware. In *The Guardian*, Gervais commented that he didn't want to stray too far from the Slough setting of his previous series – this time the main character was from Wokingham, several miles down the road. 'He has to be because I don't want to do accents. I don't want to put a wig on or do a funny walk. It's that Footlights thing; everyone talking too loud. I think recognition is always funnier. A funny face has to be earned by honesty.'

After his cameo as Oggy in the second series of *The Office*, Stephen Merchant finally bagged himself a bigger role, playing Millman's ineffectual agent Darren Lamb, while best friend Maggie Jacobs was played by Ashley Jensen, an actress from Annan near Dumfries in south-west Scotland. Initially, Jensen worked exclusively on the stage at such venues as the Citizens' Theatre in Glasgow and the Traverse in Edinburgh. She had then worked her way up through TV series such as *Rab C. Nesbitt, Bad Boys, Casualty* and *Dangerfield,* as well as the occasional quality Brit flick like *Topsy-Turvy* and *A Cock and Bull Story.*

She was called back no fewer than five times by Gervais and Merchant before they gave her the part, as she told BBC America: 'First of all I went to see Charlie [Hanson] the producer on the Tuesday. I had a few scenes that the guys had written that I read for Charlie. And he then and there said, "Why don't you keep hold of the scripts and come and meet Ricky and Steve on Friday?" So I did and I read with Ricky on the Friday afternoon, and then found out later that day that they wanted to see me again the next week, so they sent a few more scenes to read. So that was kind of ten days.

'Then the weekend from the Friday to the Monday was the longest weekend in the world. I did the last interview at three o'clock Friday and found out at twelve o'clock on the Monday. So it was a very long weekend, that one, waiting to see if I had the job or not.' The delay underlines the duo's painstaking analysis of personal chemistry, ensuring the human jigsaws on which their shows' success depend produce the perfect picture.

Talking about how the characters played off against each other, Merchant commented that he and Ricky 'are very fond of Laurel and Hardy and Morecambe and Wise. We decided to incorporate that double-act thing into the show . . . which gives Ricky the chance to play the straight guy for a change.'

Maggie doesn't have the aspirations that Andy has – she's a reasonably straightforward person who uses her time on and off set to check out possible boyfriend material – and, in a David Brent-ian kind of way, always manages to make a terrible faux pas with potential lovers.

On the back of *The Office*'s outstanding success, the BBC wanted Gervais's latest series to go out on prime-time BBC1 as the highlight of its autumn 2005 viewing schedule. But the comedian and his team were naturally protective about their latest project and stuck to their guns to give it the same low-profile launch as its predecessor had enjoyed. 'All my favourite things have started off as intimate,' Ricky reasoned. 'Nothing I like is particularly populist. If something gets big, fine.'

Warming to his theme, he explained to *The Observer*, 'It's not getting ten million viewers that's the problem; it's aiming for ten million. Or rather it is things that are made to be populist that disappoint and disgust me. By showing on BBC2 we have halved our audience already. We want people to choose it, not just turn it on. I don't want to sell door to door.' Corporation bosses capitulated, and the series went out on BBC2 as was his original wish.

Scheduling the final result wasn't the only headache facing the new series. At the press launch, Ricky gave reporters an insight into the difficulties of securing the services of willing but in-demand global superstars. 'I really can't believe we got away with it. It's bad enough trying to get everything co-ordinated with new actors. But when you've got people for one day who might be in the middle of a film on the other side of the world, it's amazing we pulled it off.'

The idea for the show had actually come at the last minute. Merchant and Gervais already had three other workable concepts in mind for a follow-up to *The Office*. (One was *Men at the Pru,* a sitcom about 'a group of twenty-somethings in a seaside town in 1970' that had more than a whiff of *The Likely Lads* about it. 'It was going to be sort of our *Billy Liar,*' said Gervais.) But *Extras* was a clear winner. 'It was just irresistible,' Ricky confided to *The Guardian,* 'the scope of it. And my favourite themes are all there: men as boys, self-delusion, vanity, all the biggies.

'We touch on my favourite sins – desperation and ego. I get more material from the egos of actors than anything else. It has always fascinated us, the way actors talk about themselves. Actors are usually, on the whole, thick, desperate, untalented and always thinking, "What about me? What about me?"'

As a latecomer to acting, Ricky's disdain for the 'luvvie' temperament had been undiminished, if not reinforced, by contact with stars and superstars. The writing of *Extras* had, in that respect, been therapeutic, as he revealed to *The Sunday Times.* 'Incompetence, people slurping in restaurants, people whistling too loud, people talking too loud, people talking inanely too loud, bad service. I've managed to put them all into *Extras,* so the show's like my own *Room 101.*'

The new venture had a lot to live up to. Mining the same rich vein of comic agony *The Office* had exploited, *Extras* also employed an effective mood-setting theme tune like its predecessor. While *The Office* had used

'Handbags and Gladrags' by Mike d'Abo, the new series dug out one of Ricky's heroes, Cat Stevens, and used one of his more obscure songs. Written and performed by Stevens in the early 1970s, 'Tea for the Tillerman' was a quirky yet apt choice.

Extras was premiered in the UK on 21 July 2005. As if to emphasize the global nature of Gervais's fame, the first episode featured a cameo by *Meet the Parents* star Ben Stiller, playing himself as an aggressive film director. Other big names lined up to appear in the series included Kate Winslet, Ross Kemp, Les Dennis, Samuel L. Jackson and Patrick Stewart – a cosmopolitan line-up of British and American actors from the small and big screens.

The series got off to a slow start. The first episode saw Millman befriend a Bosnian refugee whose real-life tragedy informed the movie that Ben Stiller was directing: it was uneven, with moments of high comedy followed by passages that were flat and totally unfunny. There were instances of full-on brutality, almost too close to the bone to be truly funny, such as the moment Stiller turns on Goran the Bosnian fugitive and shouts, 'Would you stop going on about your dead f**king wife?!'

Once again the old chestnut about Eastern Europeans liking Coca-Cola was tossed into the mix, there were jokes centring on race and cancer, and a scalpel-sharp put-down of film-buff pretentiousness in a scene at a party where talk turned to Japanese film directors. Maggie's romantic overtures to the production accountant hit rocky ground with a series of embarrassing faux pas about disability, which climaxed with a quip about the poor chap's built-up shoe looking like Herman Munster's boot. In a sense she was more David Brent than David Brent.

But the final scene, where Gervais's ill-timed, ill-informed *Starsky and Hutch* comment got him the sack, was a comic vignette ranking with the best. Ultimately, the series appeared to be revelling in the same kind of finely observed social absurdities that had made Wes Anderson films like *Rushmore, The Royal Tenenbaums* and *The Life Aquatic with Steve Zissou* such masterpieces.

The idea of landing big names wasn't just to give the series a more mainstream appeal. Merchant and Gervais wanted figures who had a certain amount of baggage that the pair could play with – people who could bring a certain weight to the programme. Their post-*Office* notoriety meant they got them, and at a cut price. 'We paid them,' quipped Ricky, 'but let me tell you – they certainly didn't do it for the money.'

Nonetheless, Gervais was very supportive of his special guests. 'When we sent Ben [Stiller] the rough idea, he sent me an email saying I'd tapped into his very soul. But he isn't like that at all. In fact he's very erudite and quite a quiet character. He was fantastic – he flew over from LA and it rained for two days. It was a great introduction to working in Britain.'

When the HBO television channel aired *Extras* in the States, reaction from the American media was far more positive and uniform than it had been for *The Office*. The series was universally well received, reviews ranging from the enthusiastic to ecstatic. *Hollywood Reporter* commented, 'Incisive, fearless and laugh-out-loud, this will appeal to anyone who liked *The Larry Sanders Show* and *Curb Your Enthusiasm*,' while the *LA Times* described it as, 'At once more modest and more ambitious than its predecessor, more focused on detail and yet more expansive. It is also excruciatingly funny, with an emphasis on excruciating.'

Press reaction in the UK was perhaps not as over the top as it had been for *The Office* – but, while comparisons were inevitable, some reviewers preferred the new offering. Gerard O'Donovan of *The Daily Telegraph* seemed pleasantly surprised by the first episode, remarking that because Gervais had 'emerged so fully formed in his new character . . . Brent was immediately subsumed into the past'. *The Guardian*'s Sam Wollaston described it as 'very funny, because Gervais is a brilliant comic actor, and he and Merchant write some pretty funny lines'. Former adversary Caitlin Moran of *The Times* was slightly less impressed, suggesting that because *Extras* was much less of an ensemble piece, 'the weight in each show is shouldered by the week's celebrity guest star, playing a cameo against type to show what great sports they are.'

However, after a slow start the show improved somewhat over the remaining five episodes. In episode two, Millman and Maggie were hired for a Second World War movie: as with the opener there were once again regular jokes about physical disability, or rather people's perceptions and reactions to it, with a recurrent jibe about cerebral palsy.

These were themes that Gervais had first started to explore in early episodes of *The Office*. As Ashley Jensen admitted to *The Independent on Sunday*, 'There were times when you read the script and thought, "Oh God, how am I going to get away with that?" But a lot of intelligent comedy does poke you a bit. It opens things up. I don't know what they're going to do for the next series, though. Because, really, we didn't leave anyone out.'

Gervais has frequently been accused of politically incorrect humour, Jim 'Nick Nick' Davidson citing his frequently un-PC gags as one reason he himself was hitting the comeback trail. But Ricky has always argued that his humour has a strong satirical element. As he explained in an interview: 'My humour isn't un-PC at all. I think it's clear there's a satirical edge to my characters, or my stand-up, even when I go under my own name. It's clearly me, getting it wrong. Playing the idiot. There's no hate involved.'

Kate Winslet – like Ricky, another export from Reading – excelled in her cameo as a Mother Superior looking for spiritual reassurance in Nazi-occupied France, revealing a fine comic side to her talents. The *Titanic* star gave Maggie advice on how to deal with her current boyfriend, who liked her to talk dirty to him on the phone, with a series of hilariously crude innuendos. Once again, there was a selection of cutting observations on actors and acting, with Winslet delivering the priceless line: 'Doing a film about the Holocaust, you're *guaranteed* an Oscar!'

In the third instalment, this time on the set of an eighteenth-century costume drama, shaven-headed tough guy Ross Kemp (Grant Mitchell of *EastEnders* fame) was called in to send up his macho image, and reputedly took offence at some of the lines he had to deliver. In among the jokes on age, diarrhoea, small breasts, the SAS (Super Army Soldiers) and pubic hairs in the catering, Kemp tried to impress Millman with stories of his hard-man past. But when dragged into a confrontation with another hard nut – ex-footballer Vinnie Jones, who was working on the next set – he revealed himself as a snivelling wimp. Meanwhile, Andy, in between struggling to find his elusive speaking part and being reduced to playing 'fourth seaman from the left', managed to put his foot in it by referring to his lead actor as a member of Spandau Ballet.

The episode of *Extras* that caused most controversy featured game-show compère Les Dennis, whose name had, at that time, been recently dragged through the gutter press due to his marital break-up with attractive (and considerably younger) actress Amanda Holden. Down-on-his-luck Dennis played Aladdin in a panto in Guildford and, for the first time, Millman got a chance to tread the boards like a real thesp, even if it was only as a camp genie.

Included was a sequence where Dennis called up celebrity-gossip magazine *Heat* to drum up his own publicity. And, in a case of art imitating real life, Les was involved with an attractive twenty-six-year-old blonde, Simone, who was seeing a stagehand on the side while taking Dennis for all he was worth. In amongst cracks about homophobia and a neat send-up of the musical *Grease*, Gervais managed to plumb new depths of pathos in a moving scene in a pub where he tried to help Dennis regain his sense of humour.

Writers Gervais and Merchant were obviously playing hard and fast with their audience's expectations. Even Gerard Kelly, who played Bunny the bisexual choreographer in the episode, expressed concerns that things had been taken a bit too far. But Les Dennis himself was happy with the result, which made it easier for Gervais to defend his tactics.

As he pointed out in *The Independent on Sunday*, 'It's the press perception of him we played with. Les isn't a sad, lonely man. Through no fault of his own he became a whipping boy.' And the former *Family Fortunes* star was quick to jump to Gervais's defence in the same paper. 'Ricky called me and said, "Look, we're writing you this part and if you're not interested let us know." And I said, "Obviously, I don't have to think twice." The script arrived on Christmas Eve. A lot of people have said, "Oh. It was so funny and you were so brave." With all Ricky's stuff, you watch it from behind a cushion. When you're in it, you watch it from behind the sofa, in the next room . . .

'I knew the implications of how dark it was. I watched it with some friends and a couple of them had to watch a second time before they felt comfortable with it. But it was Ricky and Stephen who said, "How far can we go?" and me who said, "Go all the way." There've been so many people who've taken the piss out of the situation I've had; to be seen to take the piss myself draws a line under it.'

Hollywood legend Samuel L. Jackson also cropped up in the series, albeit briefly, in the fifth episode, which was rife with cracks about racism and apartheid. Maggie, taking centre stage for once, set her sights on a black actor and, despite a series of blunders such as admitting, 'I hate reggae!', ended up pulling him. When the scene shifted to her flat, prior to making out with her date on the sofa, she has to remove a toy golliwog from her shelf. Not one to be left out, Millman also put his foot in it when, confusing Jackson with actor Laurence Fishburne, he congratulated him on his fine acting in *The Matrix*.

Jackson was another superstar keen to offer his services to the show. As he revealed in a newspaper interview, 'I started watching *The Office* when I was over in Britain and

I loved it so much I bought the first series on DVD. Ricky and I have met several times and had fun together, so when he told me about the show and what he was trying to do, I was immediately like, "OK, I can do that!" It's great to work with one of my comedy heroes.'

The subplot had Andy trying desperately to avoid a fellow extra on set and failing miserably. Following a sequence of entertaining scenes where Millman attempted to give this lonely hanger-on the slip, there was a beautifully observed moment in a restaurant where his pursuer produced two tickets for the musical *We Will Rock You*, and a defeated Millman fell face-down in his soup.

Millman's dreams appeared to come true in the final instalment, which saw Patrick Stewart rise to the occasion. In among the obvious *Star Trek* jokes, there was an hilarious scene where Andy entered Stewart's trailer on set and pitched his script to the bald-headed Shakespearean actor and one-time captain of the *Enterprise* in a welter of sexist innuendo.

Stewart found filming *Extras* 'the most civilized job I have had for years,' as he explained in *The Independent on Sunday*. 'Clever script, sensitive direction. Congenial hours, comfortable car, soap and towel in the dressing room. The only problem was Ricky, who shrieked with laughter at everything I said on camera until I began to think that I was funny – or, of course, terrible – and that is nothing to laugh about. Everything about this job was a startling new experience for me.'

What was especially clever was the subtle way in which Gervais and Merchant drew freely from their own experiences in getting *The Office* commissioned and weaved them into the script. The scene where Millman and his agent meet with the Head of Comedy and script editor was a wonderful spoof of a real-life situation and was actually set in BBC Head of Comedy Jon Plowman's office at the BBC's White City complex. Actor Jude Law was rumoured to be appearing in the final episode, but the star reputedly pulled out at the last minute. The closest he got was to have his face on a poster for *Alfie* on the wall of the studio back lot.

Although rewards were fewer on the ground than they had been for *The Office*, fortunes would change in Lucerne, Switzerland, at the annual Rose d'Or Light Entertainment Festival for entertainment television programming in April 2006. *Extras* racked up two awards for Best Sitcom and Best Sitcom Actress for Ashley Jensen. Even more gratifying must have been the Honorary Rose d'Or that Ricky won for his 'Exceptional Contribution to the Global Entertainment Business'. Jensen had already been rewarded for her comic efforts when she received two trophies at the 2005 British Comedy Awards for Best Actress and Best Comedy Newcomer.

Extras hadn't even been broadcast when Ricky did a spot at the Live 8 concert in London's Hyde Park on Saturday 2 July in front of 150,000 people, but it offered the perfect opportunity for stars like Madonna and Brad Pitt to offer their services for the second series. 'Brad came up to me and said he loved *The Office*, so I asked if he wanted to be in *Extras*,' said Gervais. 'He said, "Call me,"' though co-writer Merchant added, 'I don't think that counts as a yes. I think he was just being polite.'

Gervais's appearance on stage at Live 8 alongside the likes of U2, Robbie Williams, REM and Angelina Jolie had been much anticipated. But it sparked controversy when, in typically provocative mode, Ricky rushed on stage to announce, seemingly spontaneously, that G8 leaders Tony Blair and George W. Bush had quadrupled aid for the developing world and there was no point in continuing the show.

Someone who didn't see the joke was Live 8 co-producer Richard Curtis. Despite having been previously so complimentary about *The Office*, the *Four Weddings and a Funeral* writer was furious. There's little doubt which of those ceremonies he would have liked to plan for a man he claimed 'doesn't know his arse from his elbow'. Reported in the *Sunday Mirror*, Curtis was quoted as saying, 'He was using world poverty for a gag. I don't know who invited him here.' However, the man from Reading redeemed himself when, before introducing REM, he thrilled the massed audience by doing something he'd claimed he'd never do and reprised his hilarious monkey dance from *The Office*.

Interestingly, the subject of whether he would 'do a turn at Live 8', if asked, had come up several months before in a magazine interview with *Time Out*'s Graham Wray. Explaining how he'd approach the gig, he revealed, 'I'd have to do my own brand of comedy. I'd go out and say, "It's good to do a concert for the poor. And by the look of you lot, most of you are homeless as well."'

He'd also suggested a joke at the expense of Phil Collins. 'We're still trying to break records on the twentieth anniversary of Live Aid. I've just heard Bob Geldof has put Phil Collins on a jet to Philadelphia. There's nothing going on there, we just don't want the bald twat around this year . . . No. I'm joking, of course we didn't put him on a jet. We stuck him in a catapult. To be fair, he didn't get very far. Although it worked in rehearsals when we used it on Chris De Burgh. I could do a whole routine about injuring Phil f**king Collins . . .'

The end of yet another incident-packed year saw the release of what would become a broadcasting phenomenon – the first in a series of podcasts. Back in 2001, undoubtedly on the back of the success of *The Office*, Xfm had re-employed its former presenter to host a new radio show and gave him carte blanche 'to say whatever he wants'. He was partnered, naturally, by Stephen Merchant, but they would also find themselves working alongside the unique talents of Karl Pilkington. The Mancunian graduated from simply producing their radio show to becoming a contributor of various wacky strands and, from late 2005, a participant in their successful podcasts.

Ricky has dubbed Karl Pilkington 'genuinely the funniest man in the world . . . That man is my Homer Simpson.' High praise indeed for the former Xfm radio show producer who, legend has it, asked for a digital camera as a leaving present when he left his producing job at the station. On being presented with the gift-wrapped camera at his leaving party, he refused to open it because he wanted to give it to his girlfriend!

The deadpan Pilkington grew up in Manchester and received a rather unusual education as his parents regularly took him out of school during term time to go on caravanning holidays – Ricky would have *loved* that!

However, Karl once admitted that he had received an award from school for attendance, though he reckoned this was a device to make him spend more time in class. Talking about his lack of education and qualifications, he once admitted, 'I haven't got that much. I'm all right, aren't I?' Among his strongest childhood memories were the time he spontaneously played the drums on 'Little Donkey' during a nativity play, and his pet magpie, Maggie, which flew away when he took it into school to show his mates.

Karl's anecdotes about his family regularly entertained both Ricky and Stephen. His brother was supposedly thrown out of the army for driving his tank to the corner shop to buy cigarettes, while his dad apparently once crashed a train at Piccadilly Station in Manchester. As well as his magpie, Karl kept other pets, notably cats, one of which his mum shaved after it was repeatedly sick!

Pilkington has strange views on a whole series of topics, but he is particularly obsessed with 'freaks' – his Cheeky Freak of the Week became a regular feature on Xfm, while his favourite film is *The Elephant Man*. He believes his baldness may have been caused by his having to work a twenty-four-hour shift supervising the production of audio-cassettes – or more likely from poor cutting by a local barber who used to cut his hair in a shack near his local railway station when he was a youngster.

The wacky addition of Pilkington to the mix added a new dimension to their shows, and from this grew their podcast activities. Essentially, a podcast is an audio programme that can be downloaded from the internet on to a computer or MP3 player, and the genesis of this idea had sprung from the constraints of working for a commercial radio station. As Ricky explained, 'A wrong word now could see the station fined – but a podcast gives us free rein. It's a step forward in broadcasting, protecting creativity without adverts, ratings or radio authority.'

The podcasts were advertised as 'a half-hour of new chat each week exclusively online', and, rather than a three-way stand-up act, were akin to eavesdropping on a bar-stool conversation between friends. When they were first launched in December 2005 on the *Guardian Unlimited* website, they attracted an unbelievable wave of interest and attention. Their popularity averaged nearly 262,000 downloads a week during the first month – all absolutely free to the user, thanks to *The Guardian* paying the hosting charges.

'Karl wanted to charge a quid [for each show],' Gervais later joked, 'and now we have got five million downloads. He is gutted. He gave up his job to do this. I might give him something.' Ricky was quick to acknowledge that the concept had enjoyed a head start in the wake of *The Office*'s popularity, but as far as its content was concerned, he told the *Guardian Unlimited* website that 'We'd prefer this [the podcast] to be a few people's favourite show than a huge same-y, ineffectual broadcast.'

As a result of the venture's unparalleled success, it wasn't long before it warranted an entry in the 2007 edition of the legendary *Guinness World Records* as the world's most successful podcast, having regularly topped the iTunes podcasting chart since its launch, beating other popular contenders like cult Radio 1 DJ Chris Moyles. The comedian was subsequently honoured by

Guinness and, at the ceremony, commented: 'We had our picture taken, I got a certificate and I put it on my wall like a kid who brings home a picture. It's so great to be in it.' *Guinness World Records* editor Craig Glenday said: 'This new podcasting achievement shows there is always scope for record breaking. We're pleased to welcome Ricky and his team to the *Guinness World Records* Hall of Fame. It's got a certain ring to it: Amundsen, Armstrong, Hillary . . . Gervais.'

The radio shows on Xfm continued along the same lines, though Ricky freely admitted that little preparation went into them: 'We turn up, play records, insult Karl and go home! But it is great fun. It is a great two hours a week; three idiots shouting at each other and playing their favourite music. Perfect. What a way to spend a Saturday.'

A sentiment no doubt shared by his loyal band of listeners.

11

Crossing the Pond

> ❜ *I'm not from these parts. I'm from a little place called England. We used to run the world before you.* ❜
> GERVAIS AT THE GOLDEN GLOBES

FOR MOST MORTALS, the success of *The Office* would have been sufficient – as American singer Johnny Dowd so aptly put it, 'Be content with your life; it may not get any better.' But for Ricky Gervais in 2006, life was still getting better.

The New Year was shaping up to be even more triumphant than its predecessors had been. In a Channel 4 programme broadcast in early January, he interviewed one of his comedy heroes, Larry David, in a one-off TV special. Many miles away from his forgettable and forgotten chat-show past, *Ricky Gervais Meets . . . Larry David* was a dream fulfilled for a man who trumpeted his love of US comedy to anyone who would listen.

Larry David, though hardly a household name in the UK, had enjoyed a similarly slow-burning career as his inquisitor. Born in the Sheepshead Bay area of Brooklyn, New York, in 1947, he was an actor, writer, producer and film director. A former stand-up comedian, David had spent much of the 1980s in relative obscurity, with small parts in two Woody Allen films, *Radio Days* and *Oedipus Wrecks*. He had also written and appeared in the television series *Fridays* and contributed just one sketch to *Saturday Night Live*.

His big break had come in 1989 when he teamed up with comedian Jerry Seinfeld to create *The Seinfeld Chronicles*, later shortened to simply *Seinfeld* – a show that, after a low-key start, became one of the most successful comedy vehicles in US TV history. David appeared periodically in the show, but was never credited – and was the primary inspiration for the character George Costanza. *Seinfeld* was based on conversational and observational humour, and the premise that bad things happen to people – though the characters never appeared to learn their lesson.

In 2000, David did a special for HBO entitled *Larry David: Curb Your Enthusiasm*, and this showed such promise that, even before it aired, the channel had commissioned a series. The show was shot in a documentary style with improvised dialogue and storylines, exploring similar dark themes to *Seinfeld. Curb Your Enthusiasm* became such a hit that in 2005 David was nominated for the same Golden Globe that Ricky had won the previous year.

Gervais had been approached to participate in a series where well-known comics would talk to their comedy heroes. Ever one to shirk the spotlight, Ricky was cleverly evasive – he knew that if he asked to interview Larry David, there would be very little chance the American would agree, as he was reputedly as reticent as his Brit counterpart could be.

It wasn't difficult to see why Gervais had often cited both these American series among his favourites, including them in his top ten TV sitcoms of all time. Talking about *Seinfeld* to *Uncut* magazine, he commented, 'The first episode I saw was the 'master of my domain' one ['The Contest', on the subject of masturbation]. It was a beautiful metaphor. Nothing else needed to be said . . . That lovely symbolism. No one said c**t or f**k. They take chances, but with the structure. Deconstructing the sitcom.

'They do all that post-modern, looking-at-yourself stuff which has been done before. Since the 1930s, 1940s George Burns did it. But on *Seinfeld* they do it a little better. It's a great example of a show not aiming to get thirty million viewers, but doing everything so beautifully that you can't help but get thirty million. And Jason Alexander as George Costanza is the greatest sitcom character of all time. He carries around a picture of his "dead wife" because he thinks it will make girls like him.'

Of *Curb Your Enthusiasm*, he commented, 'I love Jewish humour . . . This is paranoia taken to the nth degree. It's the furthest out there. People who watch *The Office* sometimes say they have to watch it through their fingers, but this goes way beyond that. I have to keep mumbling "Oh God, oh God" just to get me through it. The "Beloved Aunt" episode. The golf club episode ['The 5 Wood'].

The one about the incest survivors group ['The Group'].
Unbelievable.'

Given Larry David's reclusive nature, it must have
come as a surprise to Ricky when the man behind *Seinfeld*
agreed to do the interview. The key to catching the
normally media-shy writer was *The Office*'s Stateside
success. 'Our cachet in the States had never been higher.
It had got to the point where when anyone was asked
about what they liked watching on telly they said,
"There's this British show called *The Office* . . ."'

Asked if he had been worried about interviewing one
of his heroes, Ricky replied in the negative. 'I thought,
"What's the worst that can happen? I'll annoy him." That's
never fazed me. It's sort of what I do with my friends, it's
how I make a living.' When he did meet his subject he was
pleased to note that David was 'nicer than I was expecting
and slightly nerdier, which is always pleasant. When you
meet someone who's a billionaire, and the most respected
comedy writer still writing today, it's nice to be able to see
where it comes from.' It seemed feelings were mutual as,
during the interview, Larry David commented, 'You know,
so many times when I'm watching your shows, I'm going,
"I wish *I* would have thought of that . . ."'

Still on a Stateside tip, it was also announced that Ricky
and Stephen were to write an episode for the third series
of the American version of *The Office*. Indeed, in May
2006 the *Daily Star* went further and claimed that both
Ricky and co-writer Stephen Merchant were considering a
new series, having witnessed the success of the US version.

In response, a 'source close to Gervais' was said to
have commented: 'Stephen and Ricky have been getting
sent the scripts of the US version of the show – which is

now in its third series – and falling about laughing. They're encouraged to edit the scripts, but can't find fault with them. The only thing is, they're wishing they hadn't burnt their bridges by saying they'd never do another series.'

Another US import that became popular in the UK and with Ricky was *The Simpsons*. Indeed Gervais's love of animation, and particularly American animation, had peaked with this programme. He had long been a fan of the series and, as he told *Time Out*, his first ambition when he came into comedy 'was to get a joke into *The Simpsons*'.

When questioned about his top ten favourite TV sitcoms, he said, 'It might be a cartoon, but *The Simpsons* is the best television comedy ever. It's unfair because it's almost too good. The characters are beautiful. The writing is out of this world. I sometimes sit back in amazement and wonder how they don't miss a trick. There are episodes when I've nearly been in tears, they're so beautiful and ambitious.'

So it was a huge kick for him to be invited by the show's creator Matt Groening and producer/writer Al Jean to contribute to the long-running American series. And this was after reports in the media in 2004 that the new king of British comedy had turned down an offer to go on the show because he wanted to remain in the UK. Groening had been a devoted follower of *The Office* since he first saw an episode on a plane and promptly went out and bought an English DVD player so he could watch the series.

Over the years, *The Simpsons* has seen some of the world's biggest names make cameo appearances in it, from many different walks of life: from moon-landing astronauts Buzz Aldrin and Neil Armstrong and US sporting giants like Magic Johnson and Joe Frazier, to some of Hollywood's biggest names (Meryl Streep, Dustin Hoffman, Kim Basinger and Martin Sheen). Singers like Tom Jones and Tony Bennett have appeared, not to mention rock bands as diverse as Sonic Youth and the Red Hot Chili Peppers.

But in Gervais's case, Groening went one significant step further and took the unprecedented step of asking the comic to *write* the episode in which he would star. It was the first time that a British writer had been asked to contribute to the writing of the programme since the series started in 1989. As Groening himself observed: 'It's rare we'd assign the task to somebody outside our regular staff. It's a hard show to write.'

The series producers put a call in the day after the Golden Globe awards. As Ricky told the *Sun Online*, 'It was mad as we sat down and they all quoted *The Office* to us! They asked me if I wanted to be in an episode so I said, "What are the hours?" I met the producer to talk about what we could do and he asked if I had any ideas then said, "Oh, you might as well write it!", which was incredible. I had an adrenalin rush thinking, "Oh no, what if it's rubbish?!" They liked the ideas, though.'

Recalling his encounter with Groening in *Uncut* magazine, Ricky said, 'I've never been that sort of geek or had that male autism where you know things off by heart. I never quoted *Monty Python*. But I do it with *The Simpsons*. I get with a like-minded person and I'm crying with laughter, telling them bits I remember. I met Matt Groening and I was even doing it to him. Although he just wanted to talk about *The Office*! It was a mutual back-slapping fest. I was going, "Oh, *The Simpsons* is the greatest TV show on earth," and he was saying the same about *The Office*.'

Though filled with trepidation, Gervais was soon thinking up ideas for a script – as he explained to *Sky Magazine*. 'Just think of an idea! The jokes come easier than the concept itself. I was thinking about stuff and sat down with my girlfriend and said: "Have they done a *Wife Swap* episode?" I checked with Al [Jean] and he said they hadn't, which was great for me. That's where I really see eye to eye with *The Simpsons* – it's deconstruction of telly and modern culture. The standard it has kept up is something beyond the reach of anything over here, I think. So I never got complacent and started thinking, Yeah, of course, writing *The Simpsons*. Every time I think about it I go, "Oh my God, I've written an episode of *The Simpsons*!"'

Ricky's longstanding fixation with the show also stood him in good stead. 'I don't think I know a programme better than *The Simpsons* apart from *The Office* and *Extras*. It's in my fabric. So it was great for me to write for them – it was like writing for a second series of *The Office*. I knew what all the characters were like – I could pick and choose. I just put my favourite characters in and wrote myself a nice part . . . Homer is the greatest, and I love Moe and Lenny and Carl, so they're in it. I love Chief Wiggum as well – he makes a brief appearance.'

But did the *Office* man see any parallels between himself and Homer? 'I think all men do. If you're a man and you're not like Homer Simpson, you're lacking something,' he told *Sky Magazine*. 'I love Homer because he's so vulnerable, he's lazy, he's totally dependent on Marge, he's stupid, arrogant sometimes. It's a wonderfully drawn character.'

Ricky described this episode, entitled 'Homer Simpson, This Is Your Wife', in *Time Out* as 'basically a homage to Brent. Almost an uber-Brent. Anyone who knows *The Office* will get it, but to anyone else he's just a pretentious loser . . . and I wrote a song for that episode. I've written a song for *The Simpsons*! Incredible.'

After working on the recording during 2005, the episode was broadcast in the US in March 2006 and received its first UK airing on Sky One at 6.30 p.m. on 23 April. It was preceded by a clever build-up campaign that saw Gervais making casual thirty-second appearances in between programmes, wittering on about the forthcoming episode. And prior to its Stateside broadcast, Ricky also made his seventh appearance on popular US chat programme *The David Letterman Show* to plug the upcoming *Simpsons* show.

Directed by Matthew Nastuk, the episode became a UK ratings winner, claiming Sky One's highest-ever viewing figures for a cartoon comedy. A record 2.18 million viewers tuned in to hear Ricky voice English office manager Charles Heathbar. In a magazine interview he reveals, 'He's a very normal guy who goes on *Wife Swap* with his wife. She goes to the Simpson household and thinks she's landed in cave times, and Marge comes to my house. Because she's so nice to me, I get the signals wrong, and I get drunk and sing her a love song and try to woo her away from Homer!' As for his visual depiction, he commented, 'I think they've nicely lost a few pounds, except on my top lip. I've got the *Simpsons* lip!'

It also became the channel's second most watched show following an episode of *Friends* that attracted 2.8 million viewers in 2000. The unparalleled level of its success can be gauged by the fact that a new episode of *The Simpsons* is usually watched by just over one million viewers on Sky One.

For Ricky it was a dream come true. 'Now I've written a whole script and starred in it,' he observed in *Time Out* magazine, 'I may as well retire. I went over there for the read-through and I've got Homer and Marge Simpson either side of me. I was thinking, "This isn't a career, it's like winning a competition."' He did tartly observe, however, that he was now the most hated comedian among comedians: 'They didn't mind the Globes and the other awards, but *this* . . .'

Talking about the collaboration to the press later, Matt Groening commented that Ricky was one of the most fulfilling guests that had been featured on the programme. 'He caught our tone exactly, and then added his own Ricky Gervais/David Brent patheticness. Everything you could possibly want from Ricky Gervais you get. It's possible we'll collaborate again . . . He should be a regular character. In fact he should have his own cartoon series.' Al Jean added: '[Ricky Gervais] does what people love him doing as well as fitting our universe . . . If you're a fan of his you wouldn't want to miss it.'

However, after the episode was aired, *The Simpsons* supremo publicly confessed that he was hurt that Mr Gervais hadn't picked him for a bit-part in his own *Extras* series. Despite Ricky hailing his cameo in *The Simpsons* as the pinnacle of his career, he failed to return the favour and invite Matt on to his new series of *Extras*. 'He didn't ask me,' Groening lamented to the Hollywood.com website. 'It would have been perfect for me because I worked as an extra when I first moved to Los Angeles in 1978.'

This minor hiccup aside, Gervais's Midas touch remained unblemished and offers most of us can only dream about continued to flood in on a daily basis. He was reputedly asked to play the butler to George Clooney's Magnum in the Hollywood remake of the popular 1980s TV cop show *Magnum PI*. Yet he's said that in five years' time the only place he wants to be is in a room with Stephen Merchant working on a new project.

One project he was most keen to appear in was *For Your Consideration*, a movie written and directed by Christopher Guest, known for such satirical works as *A Mighty Wind*, *Best in Show* and *Waiting for Guffman*. Guest claimed an ancestral line linking him to the British aristocracy and had enjoyed a long and happy marriage with Hollywood actress Jamie Lee Curtis. The fifty-eight-year-old comic *auteur* was a man close to Gervais's heart, as he played guitarist Nigel Tufnel in the much-loved cult heavy metal spoof, *This Is Spinal Tap*, which he co-wrote with director Rob Reiner.

Spinal Tap had long been cited by Gervais as a key influence – indeed, he believed it 'the single biggest influence on *The Office*. I saw it as a bootleg and was blown away. Whether you're in a band or working at ICI, you can relate to it. The improvisation's amazing. So many classic lines. Hysterical.'

Guest's next film was to be a satire on the Hollywood star-making machine and he had been keen for Ricky to be in it. Talking about the project in *Dazed & Confused* magazine, Guest commented, 'It's really about what happens to actors when they're told that they should win an award. They undergo a very deep psychological shift and anyone in show business is susceptible to it. If you go up to an actor and say, "I think you're good and you should win X award," that person really can't process that in a healthy way because they will immediately think that they should win. Then they'll go through this period of change where they'll think, "Well, that's ridiculous." It will go back and forth.

'This is what happens on this little movie – a ridiculous film that has no business being made, much less winning awards. The award talk becomes a virus that gets picked up by the rest of the cast, so it's true. Most actors can't process that information in a healthy way because the sort of actors that survive usually had some sort of traumatic experience when they were fourteen and decided to get love from strangers instead. It's the actors who say, "It's in my blood" who have the problems. What do you mean it's in your blood? You just mean it's better than working for a living.' Ricky would doubtless concur 100 per cent with the last sentiment.

And when the project was announced, there was the name of Ricky Gervais featured alongside those of Guest's regular stock company: Eugene Levy, Harry Shearer, Parker Posey, Fred Willard and Catherine O'Hara. Revealing how he and Gervais met, Guest observed, 'I saw *The Office* and said to my wife, "That's the funniest show I've ever seen." She told me to call him up, but I don't do things like that. Within about twenty minutes, she had called Ricky's agent and got his mobile number. So I called him and didn't get through, and then he called me back. At the time I was doing a film in London, so we met up and hit it off straight away.'

The meeting of two great minds promised great things for *For Your Consideration*. As Guest pointed out, 'The fact that Ricky is doing it makes it different to anything else I've done because he's outside the circle of people I usually work with.' The film centred around *Home For Purim*, a drama set in the 1940s American south, which is generating an award-season buzz. Gervais played the shady head of Sunfish Classic Studio's specialty division which produced the film.

Asked whether he would bring some of David Brent to the role, Ricky joked, 'I'm trying something different. I'm going to play him as an outrageously gay Jew who goes around saying [in a high-pitched voice], "Ooooh, I say, what's this then? Oooh, look at all you creatures, you make me want to *nousch*."'

A gay, Jewish David Brent? The mind boggles . . .

12

Stand Up
and Be Counted

*❛ My mum always used to say to me, "The worst thing
that could happen to you when you go to the bookies
is that you win." But I never really agreed with her. ❜*

DESPITE a clearly heavy workload in the first half of
2006, Ricky still found time to help someone who'd
given him a leg up in the early days. The first part of the
year found him treading the boards at two benefit gigs
for Nottingham comedy club Just The Tonic, which was
threatened with closure after being evicted from its long-
time location by property developers. 'When Ricky was a
budding star, appearing on *The 11 O'Clock Show*,' said
promoter/fellow comedian Darrell Martin on the
Chortle comedy website, 'he saw me doing a gig at the
Guilty Pea club (now gone) and we all went off for a

drink afterwards. He said he didn't feel he'd earned his comedy spurs, having never done stand-up. I talked him into doing a ten-minute spot in Nottingham – and that is where he did his first ever gig.

'When the problems with my club came up, Ricky offered to do a gig to help me raise some money. It was as simple as that. I texted him a few days later saying, "Can I take you up on your offer of a blatantly make-me-some-money gig." He texted back, "Yes, when?" I couldn't believe he offered to do it.'

With an episode of *The Simpsons* on the point of being broadcast in America, his genre-establishing series of podcasts already successful enough to merit an entry in the book of *Guinness World Records*, and a date at the prestigious Rose d'Or Television Festival in his diary, Ricky could have been forgiven for citing a busy schedule as reason not to get involved. Instead, a delighted Darrell Martin found himself pocketing a cool £50,000 to invest in new premises – or, according to Gervais, 'a new conservatory and a hot tub'. (Martin had offered Gervais a stake in his new club, but was magnanimously turned down.)

The events were held at the Dominion and Lyceum theatres in London on successive nights, and saw Ricky recruit pals Jimmy Carr and Robin Ince to bulk out an impressive supporting bill. Those lucky enough to get tickets to the Dominion show (the gig had sold out in an hour and a half, testament to Ricky's pulling power) had to shuffle past a larger-than-life-size cardboard cut-out of Freddie Mercury, the venue taking a day off from its usual function of staging the Ben Elton-penned musical *We Will Rock You*, based around Queen songs. Ricky may once have managed a Queen tribute band, but, despite his great love of music, it is hard to imagine him going down the Elton route in the future and becoming a twenty-first-century Tim Rice to someone else's Lloyd Webber.

The performances also represented an opportunity to dust down his stand-up act a few days before the Teenage Cancer Trust Benefit at the Royal Albert Hall in March 2006. For this, he had assembled a supporting bill that promised a rousing night's comedy – as a by-product, ensuring the success and failure of the evening would not rest on his shoulders alone. He has, indeed, been quoted as saying the only way he can do a two-hour show is to have a thirty-minute warm-up act and a long interval! But it was clear whom the audience had come to see. In the words of *Evening Standard* critic Bruce Dessau, present at the Dominion: 'He soon hit his irreverent, giggly stride . . . straddling a precarious line between political incorrectness and full-on outrage.' Some people had apparently paid up to £300 on eBay for their tickets and may have felt short-changed by a twenty-minute set from Ricky, despite the presence of Jimmy Carr and Tim Vine on the bill.

During his brief appearance on stage for the money-raising venture, Gervais feigned incredulity at the fact that he had had to pay the taxi fare from his nearby home himself: 'Six pounds down on the deal. *Unbelievable!*'

Unfortunately, not all the critics shared Dessau's enthusiasm for Ricky's part in the proceedings. *The Daily Telegraph*'s Dominic Cavendish was decidedly under-whelmed by the show at the Lyceum. 'Seldom can a household name have looked less eager to rise to the challenge of entertaining 2,000 people,' he thundered, concluding that, 'What we got resembled a hasty fag-break with David Brent.' It was true the act had drawn on topics familiar to viewers of *The 11 O'Clock Show* some six years earlier – the supposedly 'shirking' handicapped and the failure of African drought victims to move to water. But perhaps with all that was going on in his life and career he could be forgiven the occasional under-par performance now and again?

Nevertheless, having notched up a bit more stand-up experience to help out a friend in need, it was time for Ricky to turn his attention to the more serious charity venture. Comedian Russell Brand, whom Ricky asked to compere the show at the Teenage Cancer Trust Benefit gig, was a man looking to make a similar transition to the mainstream. Yet while Gervais was a master of the mundane and menial, much of the lanky, bearded Brand's act played up to his edgy, bad-boy image. A former self-confessed dabbler in the world of hard drugs, he had been sacked by MTV for turning up at work the day after 9/11 dressed as Osama Bin Laden. Though the music channel subsequently re-hired him, as Xfm had Ricky, Brand was at the other end of the entertainment spectrum from Gervais, and admitted as much by telling the Albert Hall audience, in so many words: 'Hi, I'm a star of MTV – which means ninety per cent of you won't know who I am.'

The event was the first night of the Teenage Cancer Trust's annual week of shows, organized by The Who singer Roger Daltrey, the charity's patron. And while the rest of the week would comprise bands of the stature of Judas Priest, The Cure and Goldfrapp, this 'Evening of

Sublime Stand-up' (as it was billed) was, with respect to fans of Robin Ince, Alan Carr and Sean Lock, being sold mainly on Gervais's name and star status.

Ricky claimed that, when he took Daltrey's personal phone call, he had thought it was 1970s ventriloquist Roger DeCourcey of Nookie Bear fame. Nevertheless, despite the 'disappointment', he had agreed to put together a bill of his favourite stand-ups, and duly invited a number of comedy heavyweights who appeared to meet with the approval of the ticket-buying public. And when his disembodied but eminently recognizable voice, amplified from backstage, asked the question, 'Are you ready for some comedy?', the answer from the 5,000 souls present was very much in the affirmative.

Ricky made his appearance as the third turn out of six, ambling from the wings at the behest of Russell Brand after Lee Mack and Stewart Lee had warmed up the crowd. Dressed down in black T-shirt and jeans that had clearly seen some use, he grinned nervously, the familiar facial expression magnified by a screen high above the stage. A thin film of perspiration was visible under the harsh lighting.

It was a far cry from the majority of venues where stand-up traditionally flourishes. These, he acknowledged, were usually licensed premises where the star turn was forced to take shelter in the men's conveniences that doubled as a dressing room. The Royal Albert Hall, he explained, was somewhere you don't expect to look down and see yourself standing in a puddle of urine – 'usually your own' – and thus he was in ebullient mood.

Referring to black-ink cues on the back of his hand, he rattled through jokes about French and Saunders (dubbing the former, with whom he'd crossed swords, 'the short, fat, funny one with the big ego'), ME (*not* a disease, he insisted) and his own work for 'charidee'. Should he, in the future, find himself competing for treatment with a Teenage Cancer Trust beneficiary, he joked, 'I'll say *I* paid for that machine – get the little bald f**ker out of here!'

He acknowledged his place alongside 'my favourite stand-ups' had been earned via 'my superlative TV work', which included '*The Office, Extras* and *TV's Most Embarrassing Moments*'. His twenty minutes' worth of work done, he invoked a childish nursery rhyme about the Royal Albert Hall he'd first heard back in his native Reading: 'Hitler has only got one ball – I'm off in search of the shrivelled testicle . . .' With that, he was gone.

The half-time interval, which saw a significant proportion of the audience charge outside to draw cigarette smoke into their needy lungs, also witnessed some heading off further into the darkness, unwilling to remain for the second half of the show now the star turn had been and gone. 'Well, he must have spent all of ten minutes in the dressing room coming up with that act,' said one punter to his friend. 'That's harsh,' came the rejoinder. 'Well, it certainly wasn't his A-grade material . . .' concluded the first. In their haste to leave, however, they and their fellow departees would miss a second, unscheduled appearance, when the sound on a video about the Teenage Cancer Trust malfunctioned and Ricky returned to the spotlight to save the day.

Back in the heady, if unsuccessful, days of Seona Dancing, Ricky had been asked whether his rise to 'pop fame' had been a little easy compared with the 'on-the-road graft and grind' by which fame had traditionally been attained. 'I suppose so,' he said, 'but I don't think all that stuff is relevant any more, if it ever was. We've certainly been very lucky so far. No one has yet has criticized us at all.' After that, writer Sean Thomas added the parenthetical statement, 'I shouldn't worry about that, Ricky, I'm sure it will come.'

And, of course, it did. *Extras* had not quite matched the success of *The Office*, while stand-up appearances attracted criticism that Gervais had not learned the craft. And critics complained when a man who had frequently told the press that he wasn't interested in money started to charge £5 per download for his podcasts when *The Guardian*'s sponsorship expired.

Something else that arrived unbidden on his doorstep was an excess of public attention. 'I feel slightly embarrassed even talking about this,' he'd told *The Daily Telegraph* as early as 2002. 'I don't get hassled a lot. I'm not Tom Cruise; people don't camp outside my house. It's more like: "Look, there's Ricky Gervais with a [supermarket] basket." But I'd rather be respected as a director than an actor, and I would have been just as happy not being in *The Office*.'

Being spied on while shopping was one thing, but when recognition spoilt Ricky's enjoyment of music then that was taking things too far. A night out with Jonathan Ross and wife Jane Goldman at an Oasis concert at London's Astoria in 2005 went downhill fast, the Softpedia website reported, after he was spotted in the

VIP area overlooking the dance floor. 'Someone turned around and saw me, and soon about five hundred people were chanting, "Ricky, Ricky." I thought it was quite funny. A bit embarrassing. But then somehow, within minutes, it changed into, "You fat bastard. You fat bastard."'

For Ricky, the most surreal part of the experience had been the musicality of the chanting. 'I was like, "How did *that* happen? How did they all suddenly know to chant that all together?" And they came in on the beat perfectly . . .'

It wasn't the last time he'd be on the receiving end of unwelcome attention. In May 2006 he was targeted by, of all people, students of his own alma mater. He was jogging past the UCL on a very warm afternoon when a group of students made him the target of their water balloons. 'They shouted to him, but he ignored them,' an onlooker recounted, 'so they chucked one at him to get his attention. They thought he'd see the joke, but he marched up to the door and rang the bell.'

An irate Ricky would later explain that he 'gave them a ticking off as a joke – but they looked terrified so I felt guilty afterwards'. It must have been galling to receive this unwelcome attention on his own 'manor'. Almost as irritating was a photo that appeared in the tabloids depicting a tracksuit-clad Ricky jogging near his central London home, head down, with his MP3 player guarding against all distractions, excepting that of a paparazzi lens. He did, however, appreciate the punning headline – 'iPodge' – that accompanied it.

In terms of his professional life, though, Ricky had never been in greater demand. Indeed, it was rumoured he'd turned down a potential £10 million in earnings from Hollywood alone. Having rejected 'so much money it was shocking' from the BBC to make a third series of *The Office*, he had no problem resisting the blandishments of the big screen. As well as *Magnum PI*, these had included a part alongside Al Pacino in *The Merchant of Venice*, a role in the second *Pirates of the Caribbean* movie and a cameo in TV drama *24*.

'The money being offered was criminal,' he explained to the IGN website. 'But I am not interested in money. I'm interested in doing something I am proud of. Money gives me the creeps. I hate it when people print how much I'm getting paid. It's not guilt. It's embarrassing enough being an actor for a living – it's a worthless, pointless job. But when people know you earn a thousand times what a nurse earns it's f**king embarrassing. I am not proud of my earnings. I'm proud of my work.'

Typical of his feelings was the speech he'd made in 2002 after *The Office* was voted Best Television Comedy and Gervais Best Actor at the British Comedy Awards. 'You don't know me,' he admonished the star-studded audience, 'so don't come up and congratulate me afterwards.' There was more than a grain of Gervais himself in the sentiment.

But family was different. Even with Ricky's impossible work schedule, family Christmases remained a tradition. 'I can see him now, sitting at that table, and we'll be winding each other up,' Bob recalled. 'We're always competitive, watching *Who Wants To Be a Millionaire?* and trying to beat each other.' Little brother himself has said: 'Men are children. Their competitiveness means they always have to win, even if it's a game of Trivial Pursuit.'

When Ricky returns to Reading, he can often be found supping ale in a local pub where, if approached, he is willing to meet his fans. As far as former school friend Ricky Bell was concerned, when speaking to *The Mail on Sunday*, Gervais is still 'just a friendly, affable guy. He's not very comfortable around people he doesn't know – he's shy, and the fame thing is not something he was ever interested in. He just enjoys comedy. He accepts that the fame side goes with the territory, but he doesn't go after it.

'Ricky is not full of himself at all – he wouldn't let himself change, and nor would his brother Bob. They are always giving each other stick. When Bob is in a group, he performs more than Ricky does, though. It runs in the family!'

It's certain that Bob was a strong influence on the young Ricky. Indeed, he has jokingly nominated himself as the inspiration for much of his little brother's comedy. When asked if he recognized his own jokes in *The Office*, he replied with a laugh: 'Yeah – all of them.' While his daughter Nicole has loyally insisted, 'My dad is funnier than Uncle Ricky.'

In late June 2006 came news that Ricky's next project would be something with which his younger fans would be most familiar. Having spoken of turning *Flanimals* into a movie, he had achieved an arguably greater coup by making a deal with ITV to turn Clunge Ambler, Grundit, Puddloflaj and friends into a small-screen series courtesy of two pioneers associated with the *Wallace & Gromit* success story.

Animation house Caramel Uncut would produce *Flanimals* in Bristol, and planned to combine traditional claymation techniques with cutting-edge computer-generated effects. Charles Mills and Terry Brain, whose previous triumphs had included *Chicken Run* and *Wallace & Gromit: Curse of the Were-Rabbit,* were to direct the series.

The six thirty-minute episodes would be voiced by Ricky himself. And ITV supremo Michael Jackson was clearly delighted that a man hitherto linked with the BBC would line up on his 'side'. 'This will go into the primetime schedule; it's not just a children's show,' said Jackson of Ricky's first major TV project since *Extras.* He added, doubtless to the BBC's increased chagrin, that he hoped the relationship would extend to further projects. It hadn't been long since Ricky had turned down a £5 million 'golden handcuffs' contract with the Beeb, quipping, 'I don't want to be the BBC's bitch.'

With the animated series expected to air by the end of 2007, it was timely that a third volume dedicated to these imaginary creatures was set to hit the shops in October 2006, just in time for the Christmas market. *Flanimals of the Deep* featured a whole new herd of these bizarre creatures, described in a press release as: 'Lurking, deep down below where the other Flanimals are, is a whole new land, just waiting to be studied and explored.

'Here, the unique, complex and completely mental life form discovered in books one and two just gets even weirder. And more fantastic. So if you feel well enough, read on and prepare to be astounded all over again. As all life started in the water, this book shows the greatest diversity of Flanimal life so far. From the lowly Mulgi and Flambols up to the more advanced creatures such as Bif Uddlers and Mulons.'

As well as the *Flanimals* announcement, June 2006 saw

filming begin on the long-anticipated second series of *Extras*. It looked like Gervais had finally managed to persuade Coldplay singer Chris Martin, whom he interviewed in *Q* magazine, to put in an appearance, though Martin had earlier claimed he turned down a role because, when watching Steven Spielberg's *Hook*, which featured future wife Gwyneth Paltrow, he had been distracted by the entrance of Phil Collins as a detective. 'You can't do adverts and you can't do acting if you're a singer,' he concluded.

Tom Cruise reputedly withdrew his services when he discovered he was to be a father – as did Madonna, who pulled out due to other filming commitments. Nevertheless, snagging Sir Ian McKellen, Orlando Bloom, Jonathan Ross, bespectacled *Harry Potter* star Daniel Radcliffe and David Bowie suggested that Ricky and Stephen still had plenty of irons in the fire.

Ricky had already made the acquaintance of his long-time hero Bowie, who had been such an influence on his musical tastes since his early teens. In March 2005 the pair teamed up in New York for Comic Relief – and if, for David Brent, Red Nose Day was the highlight of the year, this particular Red Nose Day saw his creator almost beside himself as he got to record a video diary with his idol of some thirty years.

'We met and became friends a couple of years ago,' Ricky revealed to the Chortle comedy website. 'He is a fan of *The Office* and we started emailing each other about music, comedy, *Pop Idol*, whatever. He is also very funny, very clever and a very nice bloke. Maybe you shouldn't refer to the Thin White Duke as a bloke. I'm more your Short Fat Duck.'

After Ben Stiller's appearance in the first series of *Extras*, Gervais found time to return the favour when he agreed to act alongside him in the movie *Night at the Museum*, a new film by *Pink Panther* director Shawn Levy about a bumbling security guard at New York's Museum of Natural History who inadvertently lets loose an ancient curse that causes the animals and insects on display to come to life and wreak havoc. Ricky joined a cast that also included Owen Wilson, Robin Williams and veteran Hollywood tough guy Ernest Borgnine.

Yet his attitude to fame remained grounded. 'Being famous is worse than I imagined,' he told *The Independent on Sunday*. 'I don't want to be lumped in with celebrities because I use celebrity as a derogatory term. I don't want to be looked at buying pants. I'm already too famous. I don't need to be this famous to be an actor or a comedian.' And this was a man who had been approached to make an appearance in one of the year's biggest blockbusters, *Mission: Impossible III*. Director J. J. Abrams was a big Gervais fan, but Ricky had turned down the part that was taken by Simon Pegg of *Spaced* fame because it clashed with the first series of *Extras*.

Saturation coverage by the media continued unabated – Ricky was the only comedian to make the *GQ* Top 200 Most Powerful Men in Britain, and when asked if he felt he was now a sex symbol the comic replied, 'I couldn't be sexy if I wanted to be. Comedy and being cool and sexy don't mix. Eric Morecambe was loved because he was a bald middle-aged man with glasses who wasn't trying to be cool.'

Life for Ricky Gervais, when not in the radio studio or on the set of one of his TV creations, is spent shuttling between his home, a top-floor flat in his beloved Bloomsbury, and his creative headquarters less than a mile away, just off Tottenham Court Road. His sparsely furnished office boasts a man-sized cardboard cut-out of Homer Simpson, but otherwise could easily be the workspace of a banker or company director. Once his working day is done, he likes to 'go home and watch [game show] *Deal Or No Deal.* I'm in my pyjamas by six. We eat, we open a bottle of wine . . . We dread it when we have to go out. I've been working towards middle age my whole life.'

His track record so far has proved that he's more than a one-trick pony – but as to whether he'll be remembered in fifty years' time like his heroes Laurel and Hardy, for example, remains to be seen. His success so far has lain in the way he has managed to tap into the quick-fix mindset of twenty-first-century Western life. He has a keen eye for the tawdry, unremitting existence of a generation without any real vision for the future – an ostrich-like, head-in-the-sand culture in which everybody is desperate to be somebody, to have their fifteen minutes of fame, and to get it at any price.

No wonder that, even if he hates them, he draws much inspiration from the glut of TV reality shows currently masquerading as entertainment. As he himself has commented, 'I watch reality shows to hate the people in them. Desperate wannabes. What will you do for fame? Anything. I'll show my fanny and wank off a pig. Well done.' Yet critics would pose the question: 'How different are they to David Brent, Andy Millman or even Ricky Gervais himself?'

There's cruelty and ambiguity in all the best humour, but Ricky sometimes walks a very fine line between political incorrectness and downright offensiveness. Are there any real guts behind what he does or is it just playground humour? Is he part of the problem or part of the solution? Certainly, watching his stand-up shows suggests a man who has not actually stepped beyond the small-town mentality of places like Reading or Slough – often they're a dangerous celebration of the kind of brainless, brutal toilet humour of his youthful heroes Derek and Clive.

And while one of his regular targets, Ben Elton, may serve as a reminder of how a once sharply political comedian can end up just like the target of his early jokes, the deliberately apolitical Gervais risks falling between a number of stools. He has none of the clowning facetiousness of a Harry Enfield or Paul Whitehouse, who are the twenty-first-century inheritors of British music-hall tradition, nor will he ever be able to rival the wholesome family entertainment of Morecambe and Wise or even Ant and Dec, all of whom he has expressed admiration for.

Whether translating *Flanimals* to the small screen will derail his productive partnership with Stephen Merchant is another imponderable. Yet just as his partner's future may well lie behind the camera, so Ricky will have to consider how often his audience can suspend belief as Gervais becomes Brent becomes Millman becomes . . . While he was granted the opportunity to deliver his first two major comic creations to screen himself, this may not be a luxury he enjoys indefinitely, even if the ideas keep on coming.

Having crammed so much into the last six years – radio presenting, script-writing, stand-up comedy, acting, directing, writing children's books, voice-over work, pod-casts – it's impossible to predict which way he'll turn next. But whatever happens in the future, he's certain to make the most of the fame he now has that he so eagerly sought in his younger days: 'It all came along by chance,' he told Veronica Lee of *The Daily Telegraph* in 2005, 'and then I realized I had a lot of stuff to say, just like everyone does. At the moment I have the opportunity, I just haven't got the years . . .'

In an industry where image is all, Ricky Gervais is everyman. The common touch has served him well so far. Indeed the fact that he rubbed shoulders with his hero as an equal, when an eager David Bowie was enrolled to take part in the second series of *Extras*, was yet further confirmation of his irresistible pulling power in the circles of the rich and famous. His success story has proved as unlikely as it has inspirational.

In contrast to the modern phenomenon of *Big Brother*-style celebrity culture, where individuals are turned from zeros into heroes at the drop of a hat, Ricky Gervais has earned fame and fortune through his own efforts in a myriad different ways. Whether he will prove to be a product of the zeitgeist or a truly universal figure whose humour and talents will still be celebrated a hundred years from now, only time will tell. Though you may not see him on too many red carpets – and he certainly won't turn up to the opening of a fridge – with an extensive range of talents at his disposal, his name is surely likely to remain in lights for some time to come.

Index

INDEX

INDEX